WHAT PEOPLE

THE DEEP HEART OF WITCHCRAFT

David Salisbury is well poised to lead the Millennial Generation into deeper contact with their spiritual natures. A dedicated practitioner, he writes of his encounters with the sacred in an intimate way that is sure to help new seekers along the way.
T. Thorn Coyle, mentor, activist, teacher, and author of *Make Magic of Your Life: Passion, Purpose, and the Power of Desire, Kissing the Limitless*, and *Evolutionary Witchcraft*.

A powerful and practical manual to bring the depth of spirit to your Craft.
Christopher Penczak, Co-Founder of the Temple of Witchcraft

With an inviting and engaging style David Salisbury opens the reader to *The Deep Heart of Witchcraft*. From what appears at first to be an eclectic Wiccan outline emerges a conversation that moves passed commonly accepted paradigms and provides powerfully-effective technique and meditation. I recommend this book to Witches who are eager to create and consolidate personal pathways of daily practice. Salisbury opens the door to enriching and soulful connection with the Divine.
Gede Parma, author of *Ecstatic Witchcraft* and *Spirited*

David Salisbury has written a truly brilliant work of magic, one that will take the reader on a journey deep into the hidden secrets of the elements of Air, Fire, Water, Earth, and Spirit, and explore their connection to the tools, rituals, meditations, and deities that Witches work with every day. I found myself looking at these energies in new ways and am excited to try the practices woven throughout. While many books gloss over these components in a cursory fashion, Salisbury shows how they form the foundation of a truly magical life.

Christian Day, author of *The Witches' Book of the Dead* (Weiser, 2011)

David Salisbury has written a solid, practical guide full of exercises and wisdom that will serve both the beginner and the experienced witch well. *The Deep Heart of Witchcraft* is both approachable and understandable. Covering everything from meditation to prayer, magic, to honoring the dead, Mr. Salisbury's gentle, easy style makes this a delightful addition to one's bookshelf.

Galina Krasskova, author of *Exploring the Northern Tradition* and *Essays in Modern Heathenry*

The Deep Heart of Witchcraft

Expanding the Core of
Magickal Practice

The Deep Heart of Witchcraft

Expanding the Core of
Magickal Practice

David Salisbury

MOON
BOOKS

Winchester, UK
Washington, USA

First published by Moon Books, 2013
Moon Books is an imprint of John Hunt Publishing Ltd., Laurel House, Station Approach,
Alresford, Hants, SO24 9JH, UK
office1@jhpbooks.net
www.johnhuntpublishing.com
www.moon-books.net

For distributor details and how to order please visit the 'Ordering' section on our website.

Text copyright: David Salisbury 2012

ISBN: 978 1 78099 920 3

A CIP catalogue record for this book is available from the British Library.

Design: Stuart Davies

Printed in the USA by Edwards Brothers Malloy

We operate a distinctive and ethical publishing philosophy in all
areas of our business, from our global network of authors to
production and worldwide distribution.

CONTENTS

Acknowledgements

Thank you to the many people in my life who supported this work and encouraged its completion. My mother Carol Salisbury and my partner Mike Brazell have always given me unceasing support in all that I do. Thanks to all those who believed in my work early on; Melanie Hope Smith, the Reynolds family (Jen, Debbie, and Katie), Nila Latimore, Kelsey Gibb, Kelly Kresconko, Holly Coggins, Peter Dybing, Devin Hunter, Cara Schulz, Iris Firemoon, and everyone at The Firefly House.

And finally to Nikie Little who is the reason I'm at the place I'm at in my Craft.

Foreword

The Deep Heart of Witchcraft is a book about transformation by pushing the Self through the elements, communing with the divine, and the cycles of the seasons. It encourages readers to push themselves to not just learn about Witchcraft, but to make it a daily part of life. This book will take you from being someone who is reading a book about Witchcraft into someone who is living Witchcraft. David doesn't just tell you about Witchcraft, but he encourages you to live it, breathe it, and be it. You will constantly be putting this book down, not because it's boring, but because you need to use your hands to do something. To do Witchcraft. To be Witchcraft. To live Witchcraft. David has truly crafted a journey deep into the heart of Witchcraft. I have had a first row seat to much of the continuing metamorphosis of David Salisbury that has led to this work. I founded The Firefly House, a nature-based church and school, and as a student of mine, David adapted what I had to offer into his own extensive pool of knowledge. David is one of the most talented and gifted people that I have had the pleasure to work with on my own journey. We have organized hundreds of events together, including public rituals, Pagan Pride Days, and masquerades. In supporting some of the most important national Pagan endeavors of our time, we have felt as if we were fighting for our lives, left energetically bruised and broken in the middle of the street, and yet we still manage to pull ourselves up and put one foot in front of the other. David is the kind of person who can stand in a massive spiritual tidal wave and not let his balance waiver for one moment, and this book illustrates how you can use your own will and cultivate your own inner strength. When we think that we cannot take anymore, and the Universe decides to pile that last straw that would have broken the camel's back, the principles shared in this book transform us into the kind of people who can turn "please, no more" into "bring it on, you can't take me down." Witchcraft is not just the way we commune with the divine, but it is the source of our strength as human beings, and the pages of this book provide a guide to manifest that strength within ourselves. David has studied and practiced a wide range of traditional and eclectic teachings in Witchcraft. His motive to write is to serve others, to share with others some of the musings from his own path in hopes that his experiences will help others on their own. Instead of writing from the teachings of a specific tradition, David shares teachings from his own soul. These tools are experiences that have provided growth in his darkest hour and transformation when he wasn't sure where to go next. They have given him strength to keep moving forward. They have honed his skills as a Witch. For several years, David has held many leadership roles in the local DC Pagan and national Pagan communities. Outside of learning from books and teachers, he has often had a trial by fire, so his teachings come from experience. There is no better teacher than one who has put his knowledge to the test, fallen down, and gotten back up to be a better leader. All of our leaders do fall down, and the ones who are still standing are the stronger ones, because they picked themselves back up and kept moving forward. Our authors and teachers need to be people who push themselves to be better, do more, and learn more in their Craft. David is one such person. He is constantly learning and constantly growing. Some of our most notable Pagan authors talk about their past work in a cloud of disconnection. They themselves have evolved and no longer practice or connect with what they penned a decade ago or more, because they, too, are constantly changing and learning. They are pushing themselves to be better, do more, and learn more in their Craft. And, David is one of those authors that will have trans-formed even more as he continues to push himself to new heights. Here, he pushes you, too. To be better, do more, and learn more in your Craft. For you, he forges a path of intense spiritual exploration and growth. Within these pages are tools for you to herald your own incredible transformation. Bright blessings on your path.

Iris Firemoon
High Priestess, The Firefly House

Please read banned books

Introduction

Witchcraft is work. And let's not kid ourselves, it's tough work. Any experienced Witch will tell you that to really get anything of substance out of the Craft, you have to put effort into it. You have to give it your all. When Witches set out to do something that's effective, they know that they have to put work into it on a mental, emotional, physical and spiritual level. Well, we try to anyway. We know that as magick workers, our ability to change our lives and the world around us is immediate. There is always something we can do. Notice I say *can* do, not necessarily *want* to do.

When a need arises in my life, a series of internal events occur. The first, desire, seems to be at the core of it. When I experience need (or want for that matter), the emotion of desire swells up like a wave tugging at my insides to bring it into being. Next comes will. Out of desire, I draw forth the will I need to do the work to bring my need into being. I set the choices in motion and begin work on the action. Action then becomes the next step. What actions will I take to fulfill my need? If I'm being a wise successful magick worker, I'll take any and every action that I can. What comes next? Experience. Whether or not my need came to being is beside the point. I will either have the experience of my need being fulfilled or I won't. Either way, there is a result, one that I had a hand in making happen.

Seems exhausting, doesn't it? This series of events occurs over and over again. Is it because our human "need for need" is insatiable? Perhaps. But when we take a role in co-creating our world, we experience presence. We get to the core and heart of what we're put on this planet to do, our Great Work. The more we take part in the daily creation of our lives, the more something changes within us. No longer are we bystanders or critics watching the movie of our lives play before our eyes. We are the actors. The musicians of the greatest symphony in the history of the universe.

Now, I know what you're thinking. "My life is hardly that colorful." But really, it can be. Every moment we take a breath we have an opportunity to experience presence. To me, presence means that I can not only do the work I have to do in the world, but I can take joy in it. I can face every day knowing that my full attention is right here, in my center, tapping into all the power I need. When I'm tapped into power, everything becomes possible. My heart is open to possibility when I'm experiencing presence. And that to me is what the deepest heart of Witchcraft brings us.

The question we then ask ourselves is "how do we get there?" Living a magickal life is part of it, a large part. But I'm a firm believer that like any art, practice makes perfect. When fine-tuned, developing a consistent and effective sitting practice can be one of the most transformative things one can do in their Craft career. You've read the books, you've done the seasonal festivities and you've laid a successful foundation of your practice. The real work begins when you dig deeper. This is the time when you carve out of yourself the things in your life that aren't serving you best. We fill that cavern with a toolbox of exercises and activities that sustain and nourish our life force. As magick workers, we shouldn't be interested in sameness, only what is better.

How this book works

As you read this book, you'll be taken on a journey through the classical elements of Witchcraft: air, fire, water, earth and spirit (or aether). Each element will be thought of as a "mile marker" of sorts. A guide post to help define and explore the mysteries as we deepen our practice and reach further into ourselves and our work than we ever have before. Each element is a point on the pentacle as well as the circle that surrounds it. It's a symbol. They're keys that we'll use to unlock our magickal potential.

We already know that symbols are an extremely important

part of any tradition within Witchcraft. The energy current built up behind a practiced symbol over time is of great use to the magick worker. When unlocked, the symbols aid us in tapping into a stream of power. A power that's been added to every time magick workers of the past used it. This power has been called the *egregore*, the "collective unconscious" of the magickal world. It's an autonomous energy that is alive within everything, yet displays itself differently through every symbol.

The pentacle itself is perhaps the most well known symbol of Witchcraft, with an egregore that possibly stretches as far back as the first people who looked upon the stars in the sky with wonder and awe. We are all made of stars. The particles within us that expand, move, shift and shape are the same as those inherent within the gassy masses that make up star forms. What better symbol to use for expanding our spiritual work as Witches and being fully present magickal beings?

Throughout the book you'll come across exercises that are meant to go along with each elemental chapter. Please do all of them and take your time with each one. You don't have to add each of them to your daily practice just yet, but be sure to give each of them a try. Over time, you may like to add some of them to your daily practice schedule, to even change the exercises themselves to expand or contrast in thought or form as you grow. Go deep, and don't limit yourself to anything because it may not feel like it's working the first time. Practicing the arts is a challenge and takes patience, but patience is always well rewarded.

Keeping a magickal journal

I cannot stress enough how important it is to write things down. None of us have a perfect memory (Goddess knows I don't) and we need to be able to recall the things we do and learn. If not for the sake of memory, then we at least need to write things down because it commits it to the forefront of our consciousness. When we write something down, we're affirming the thought in our heads to the physical world, bringing it into being. In that sense, every act of writing is an act of magick and should be treated as such.

Start today, right now as you're reading this if possible. If you don't have a blank book yet, start jotting things down on pieces of scrap paper until you get one to copy it into. Feel free to have fun with it. Mine is decorated with all sorts of gems and colors. It helps activate my creative mind and motivates me to keep adding to it. You don't need to add anything and everything to it, though I encourage you to do so if that's what you want. At the least, write down the exercises and the results you have with them. You'll want to refer back to them at a later time when you've been doing them for a while. It's great to be able to check in periodically and see where you're practice was when you started and where you are now. Remember how we talked about symbols as mile markers? Your magickal journal is one of those too.

Now that you've got an understanding of what we'll be doing and how to do it, let's jump in!

Chapter I

Air

*And forget not that the Earth delights to feel your bare feet
and the winds long to play with your hair.*
- Kahlil Gibran **Practicing movement**

Air brings the gifts of movement and change. Made manifest by
the forces of the eastern winds, air makes itself known in every
breath we take whether we're conscious of it or not. Air isn't
concerned about the things we think we need to make us feel
comfortable and safe. If it had its way, air would blow everything
away from us, just to show us that it can. That's the playful faerie
aspect of the air elementals, who glide seamlessly on the hems of
our thoughts, touching our ideas and gifting us with subtle
insights.

When we are present with air, we gain wings. We know that
the entire world is there for us to explore. Air expands our sense
of self in the mind and is the first way that we tap into the
egregore. The kiss of the wind knows which caverns to swirl
through to make a whistle.

With air, we can create music and place ourselves in harmony
with the things we need to take each step on our path. The wand
is the tool of air, directing our spirit allies in the orchestra of our
spells. The wand is a tool of intellect, helping us to extend our
reaches to the heavens above. Truly a unique gift to the magick
worker. When we raise our wands to the sky, we're announcing
that movement within and around us is about to begin. When
working with the power of air and movement, we're doing
mercurial work, or workings that relate to the realm of Mercury,
god and planet of travel and communication. The wand is a tool
that Mercury uses to gain passage to the destination of his

choosing. For Mercury is the only deity in the Greek pantheon who is allowed to travel to all places, known and unknown by human or god. Working with the mercurial energies allows us to open to gates of possibility. The wand is the "key" we use to open doors previously closed to us. When we open the gates of possibility, we realize that our true potential is limitless.

Exercise – Dedicating your wand

If you don't already have a wand, it's very easy to make one. Simply take a fallen branch of your choosing and cut off a length that extends from your elbow to your middle finger. I don't feel the type of wood you choose matters so much as how the wood chooses you, but feel free to use any of the traditional power woods associated with the wand such as willow, oak, ash, maple or birch. If you already own a wand, then you're good to go for the next part of the activity.

Take the wand to some wild place in nature (preferably) or to the sacred space in your home. Create your personal ritual setting and enter a meditative state. The only tool you need for this is the wand itself, but you can add any oils, candles or scents to this working that you like. Remember though that our focus for this work is connecting with your wand and the mercurial air associated with it.

Once in a meditative state, grip the wand lightly with both hands with your eyes closed. Take a series of deep in and out breaths, being particularly aware of how your breath circulates and moves through your body as it passes in and out. Notice the expanding and contracting of your chest and belly. Feel the breath as pure wind moving through your being. With continued mindful breathing, contemplate the symbols that the wand and its airy ruler present you with. Perhaps you come to a vision of a tall hilltop with puffy clouds passing overhead. Maybe you imagine yourself in a race with Mercury himself, the wand in your hand giving you a magickal boost of speed to race through the sky and across the land. Open yourself to creativity, another gift of air. In addition to any visions, notice any feelings or words that come to mind. Language and speech is probably one of the most useful air tools that the human race has. What words connect you with this energy? What types of sentences or messages are these words creating for you as you do this work? Is nothing coming to mind at all? That's perfectly fine too. It could be that the mind is telling you that the most useful thing you can do in that moment is to just sit with yourself in silent nothingness.

When you feel you're done, thank the air elementals for any visions you may have received and wrap up the wand for future use. Some believe that it's fine for the wand to be exposed as long as it doesn't touch the ground. Some believe its fine for it to touch the ground as long as it's not exposed. In the end, do what feels right for your own wand. It is now an extension of you and only you can know what's right for it.

Showing up for practice

When we want to touch the deep heart of Witchcraft, the first thing we need to do is commit ourselves to showing up for our magickal work. This is the work of deepening our connection with our souls and the divine so it's important that we actually take the time to do it and do it with some consistency. As you begin deep daily work, there's no need to over extend yourself. Five to ten minutes a day for a while is enough. It's like joining a new gym. If I haven't worked out for a long time, it means my muscles are cold and unused. They need to warm up a bit before they get to the heavy stuff. Some light cardio, maybe some cycling and running each morning but nothing big. When my body is used to it, I can start adding strength training, heavier cardio, and more advanced stretching to my workout routine. Eventually, my body will become a lean mean machine capable of the greatest athletic feats (hey, a guy can dream can't he?).

That's what we want to do with our spirits. We can't dive right into the full current of the egregore and expect to keep to the surface. We need to test the waters of where we are first.

Making a statement about showing up for practice is the first step into making your work a reality. Some people like to consider it a "personal contract" that they make with their Higher Selves or gods. I don't think it always needs to be that formal but if that's what helps you stick with it, then by all means draft up a contract. If you go that route, then I recommend you ritualize it to add a bit of magickal oomph. Create and sign the contract during a ritual and "put your money where your mouth is." When I make statements like this to my gods, its touches the deepest parts of me and changes it from something that I feel like I have to do, into something that I feel like I need to do. We're employing our will here and the gods and our higher selves will listen. When we proclaim "I'm here and I am going to do this work!" the universe will respond with support and strength. The gods want us to succeed in this work, so don't be afraid to communicate with them about the work of the practice itself.

For now, let's commit to ten minutes a day while we work with the element of air. Ten minutes may not seem anything to some people, but have you ever tried getting a busy businessman to sit still for ten minutes without falling asleep? It's no easy task let me tell you. So as we work on our exercises, we add them to our daily practice schedule. When you continue your work around the pentacle, you may want to add some things or drop some things once you develop a sense of what is making you feel more connected with your work. Our schedules are meant to change, just like our lives do.

Prayer work – your highest communication

Some Pagans have a funny way of looking at prayer. I know I did when I first started practicing the Craft. Prayer to me felt like something "those Christians do" and I wasn't interested in having any part of that. I felt like prayer was something that people did to thank God when things went their way, and then to complain to God when things didn't. Oh how wrong I was. I fought formal prayer work for years until I started incorporating it more into my practice and gained a better understanding of what it truly is. Prayer is the language we're speaking when we're talking to the Gods. Whether it's a 2,000 year old prayer in Hindi or a modern chat with the Goddess that you make up on the fly, prayer to the divine gets translated into its own special language by the higher self. Once we learn this language, we come into better communication with our gods and in turn, the Gods communicate back. I believe this is one of the core needs that all religions seek to fulfill. They seek Divine Communication.

But how is it done? Everyone seems to have their own opinion on the "right way" to pray, as if it were some exact science that only certain people are privileged enough to learn. Many religious organizations in the past and present have been very insistent on having human intermediaries to pray with. They profess that some people either need to have their prayers spoken for them, or they need to learn the "right way" to pray through them first. In most forms of Paganism and in particular Witchcraft, we believe that such ideas are preposterous. We need no intermediaries. As a pantheistic faith, we believe that God rests within all things, including ourselves. And if God resides within us, then there is no need for an intermediary because every expression we perform is connected to the Divine Mind. And this is also how prayer works. When we are in true communication with the Divine Mind, the way you pray doesn't matter. The only thing that matters is that you do it, and you do it often. I don't want to tell you that this is a "use it or lose it" scenario but it is the type of thing that gets more comfortable with time and more clear with frequency.

If you're a stranger to prayer work or you just don't do it

enough, you can feel like you're talking to a wall. While if you go through periods of intense prayer and then stop for a while, this "wall feeling" can feel like it goes right back up. To be in communication with the Divine Mind and our Divine Selves, we must make sure that our communication is sincere, constant and with intention. The Witch knows that he can pray anywhere and at any time within any range of situations. I do believe that there are some atmospheres that are more conducive to prayer when you'd like to get some type of answer back. This brings us to the differences between devotional prayer and interactive prayer.

Devotional prayer is the prayer of worship, gratitude, and prayer for the sake of prayer. It's often considered "one way" prayer where you're practicing your divine speech and religious expression. The Hindu mantras performed over mala beads at worship services could be considered devotional prayers. Though I believe this type of prayer is important, there is more that can be done when we open up to the idea of the Gods talking back to us. Interactive prayer does this. When I say "Gods talking back to us" I don't mean that you should expect some disembodied head to appear in your circle to impart sacred prophecy before your eyes. What I mean is simply being open to messages or signs, for the time that you pray and later on. Sometimes just the act of asking for reciprocal communication is the purest form of interactive prayer that we can do. When I'm praying for a sign or a message, I try to not be very attached to the outcome. I dedicate my prayer work to the goal of being open enough to express myself to Goddess and God, while being open to experience the expressions that they'll send back to me.

Sometimes this manifests itself in what we call clairsentience or "clear knowing" in the psychic vocabulary. You're sitting in class or at your work desk then out of nowhere the answer or a thought leading to an answer just pops up in your brain. This can be an extremely effective form of communication with the divine if you're open enough to your intuition, and emotionally detached enough from the response that you think you want. Easier said than done, right? When we approach our communication with perfect love and perfect trust, this isn't a problem. Perfect love means that no matter what you're asking for, all messages will be sent and received in the name of love. Love for your Gods and love for your own divine nature. Loving yourself and your work in the world is truly the best way to remain in correct communication with God. Perfect trust means that not just receiving an answer is enough. You have to trust that the answer or message you get back is true and correct and is only in service to your True Will, whether it's a message you want to hear or not. Have you ever seen someone get a tarot reading that they weren't happy with so they ask the reader to do it over? This is a lack of trust in the answer and is the biggest thing to overcome if we want our prayer work to be as effective as possible.

Exercise – Opening to intuition for prayer work

If you don't feel like you're in a very intuitive place in your life right now, this exercise can help. Even if you're a psychic-wiz and trust your intuition fully, renewing our commitment to being open to this power helps keep us sharp, focused, and open to giving and receiving the best speech possible with the divine.

First, develop a deep meditative state in whatever way is most effective for you. Do the breath work from exercise one but take it a step further by extending the time of inhales, holds and exhales consciously. Try breathing in by the count of seven, holding by the count of seven, exhaling by the count of seven, holding by the count of seven and then repeating. Try this seven times and you should find it pretty easy to form a deep trance-like state. In the *Temple of Witchcraft* tradition, they call this the "little death breath." When we calm the mind to its slowest possible state before trance, we're opening up our senses to the highest guidance possible.

After the little death breath, regulate your breathing to a soft yet still elongated pace. Next imagine a swirling ball of light shining brightly above you, about two feet from the top of your head. I like to imagine the light as violet which is a very psychic color for me, but you can also imagine it as a clear and sort of prism-like crystalline light. I avoid visualizing opaque white light as it can block out too many energies, whether harmful or helpful. Next, imagine the swirling ball of light slowly dripping down in a single strand of shimmering light towards the top of your head. Feel it touch the top of your head forming a new yet smaller swirling ball of light on your crown. This is the area where we're open to clairsentience. We're inviting those messages to pop into our heads as I mentioned before. It can be helpful to pick up your wand and physically tap the top of your head with it to confirm the presence of the light. You can also anoint it with a special oil or holy water. Now see the ball on your crown drip yet again down to the area between your two eyes - the area of your third eye chakra, forming another smaller ball of light there. This is the area where you're opening up to receiving visions to both your material eyes, and your mind's eye. Like before, tap this area with your wand or anoint it. Lastly, see the swirling ball on your third eye drip down again forming a third small ball of light in your solar plexus, the area just above your belly. This is the area where we're open to our most primal manifestation of intuition; the "gut feeling." Once again tap your wand or anoint this area. Sit with this for a moment and allow yourself to take note of any feelings that may arise. You very well may receive a message right there already. When you're done, you can imagine the smaller balls of light slowly fading into you, entering your bloodstream and dispersing into the cells of your body. The large ball of light two feet above your head ascends back into the higher planes with the knowledge that you can call upon it any time you need it. Be sure to ground and center yourself, releasing any excess energy from your person. Be sure to record your experiences in your magickal journal.

Now that all three of our centers of intuition are open, we're truly ready to engage in the work of interactive prayer. We're no longer just running our mouths but instead, we're opening ourselves up to listen. The Gods will take notice of this action. I believe that when we open to listening in this way, we're making a statement of respect and gratitude for the things that the divine want to express to us.

This question then arises after we learn about effective prayer: once we learn how to talk and listen, what should we say? The simple answer is "anything you want." Depending on the nature of your personal relationship with your deities, you might just have a casual conversation like they're old friends you've grown up with. This tends to be the way that most mature people I know pray. When children or someone new to their particular faith practices prayer, the conversation tends to sound more like a child talking to a parent. Certainly there isn't anything wrong with either method for as I said, the relationship you have will shape the way your prayers sound. The current state of your life and emotions will also shape your prayers. It's perfectly natural for someone whose life is in a state of great upheaval to have an angry tone in their prayer. I've had times of great distress in my life when I was practically screaming in my prayers, filled with passion and rage. Are you afraid of getting angry when you talk to the Gods? Don't be, they like it. Or at least mine do. When I'm in a place in my life where my passions are running high, I'm in a place where I'm open to divine experience. Sometimes getting pushed to the edge is just what we need to stumble and fall back into center.

Be honest and open in your prayers. Truth is a virtue governed by air. The wind makes no apologies about the direction it blows in. Whether destructive or refreshing, the air is honest about its nature and makes itself clear about what it's doing. Try to remember that in your work with prayer, on both ends giving and receiving. In addition to incorporating truth and trust in our prayer work, we also need to consider another characteristic of air: clarity. When we clearly define what we need in the moment, it's easier for the universe to manifest an outcome for us. Remember that the universe is infinitely abundant, if you know how to ask for things. You are probably already familiar with this concept in spellcraft. A spell is hardly effective if the intention is not clear and the specifics on what you're asking for aren't clearly laid out. There must be definition. This gives our prayers and spells the direction they need to take the most unobstructed path possible on their way to the planes of manifestation. When we're not clear with our intentions, we've already set up our magick to fight an uphill battle.

Though I truly believe that genuine prayers should be crafted from the heart of the Witch, keeping in mind some guidelines might help you remember to incorporate the most effective methods of opening to divine communication. You'll find that the flow of our formula is very similar to the setup of a basic spell, with a few differences.

Identify the purpose and make an affirmation or claim of power. Clearly state the desire and give thanks

The similarities to spellcraft are obvious. What's the difference then? Why not just do spells? The frequency of the prayer is much different to that of a spell. When a prayer goes out, its vibration is more subtle and gentle. Prayers open a line of communication that is often not engaged when one is working a spell. Once again, prayer opens us up for answers back. When we're praying for something we need (or think we need), we're open to divine guidance about the nature of that need, its base origin. Spells demand an outcome, no matter how pleasant and polite they're set up to be. There is nothing wrong with going after the things you want in life, but the beauty of Witchcraft is knowing that there are multiple channels to go about it. Now that we've defined the difference between spells and prayers, the question then becomes "when do I pray, and when do I work a spell?" That's up to you. But I find it helpful to always open up a conversation through prayer with the Gods before I work magick for it. In my own practice, I find that it helps manifest any later magickal working faster. I can't say I'm completely sure why it does, but it just happens that way. And when my magick doesn't manifest? Well that's where the "perfect love and perfect trust" we established earlier comes into play. Sometimes when I pray for something I want or need, the speech that I receive back from the divine makes me realize that I never wanted it or needed it at all. To me, that is the most effective magickal work of all. To receive that intuitive answer back that lets you know that it's ok for things to not always work out how you'd like them to. Surrender yourself to your higher power, and you open yourself to your own power and highest potential.

If you're still anxious about speaking prayers from the heart or writing some of your own, there's nothing wrong with using prayers from other people that call to you. In my own personal practice, the non-specific prayers I use are 90 percent written by other people. I enjoy speaking prayers that are poetic and romantic. The feeling helps me to connect to that raw emotional Goddess energy so I can plug into my soul's current quicker. Look through one of the many books on Pagan prayers and pick out the ones that call out to you the most. They should create a spark of passion within you, like when you heard your favorite song for the first time. You should select your base prayers that you'll use for the morning and night in your daily practice. This "prayer schedule" (for lack of a better term) will be the building blocks of your main daily practice.

Sample morning devotional prayer

Oh Great [Goddess, God, etc] of the morning dew
I come to you this blessed morning and confirm my sacred devotion

Through this day I stand strong in heart and mind
Through this day I walk with balance, integrity and strength
I affirm all possibilities that serve my highest good and welcome
them to my space
May I have the knowing to exercise my true will, the will to be
daring, and the darling to practice silence
My gratitude pours out upon the sacred ground I walk, onto you
Oh Great [Goddess, God, etc], I give thanks
Blessed Be

The morning prayer above contains that prayer creation system that I personally favor. The identification of purpose is there, as well as the affirmation, the desire and the statement of thanks. See how easy? There is much to criticize with this system though. Many will say that the best prayers are those that are spoken from the heart, and I agree with that. I think prayers can still be "from the heart" if you write them down ahead of time. Just because it was planned doesn't mean that it holds any less meaning. Some of the most connected prayers that have ever come out of my mouth have been those spoken in the heat of anger, joy or sadness. There is much that can be said about the energies raised in times when those emotions are intense. Like our magick, these feelings fuel our prayer and only serve to forge a deeper connection.

The message to take away from all this is to just pray. Pray often and pray for anything and everything. Your voice is important and the gods are ready to hear it.

Calling on inspiration

Inspiration is one of the most outwardly helpful gifts that the spirits of air bring us. It's the flow of creative or impassioned thought that can come from a specific thing, or from "nothing" at all. Really though, it all comes from somewhere. When we're inspired, we're really just tapping into a specific frequency of a larger stream of consciousness. When we open ourselves to inspiration, we're stepping into a creative flow that can fuel the work we do in all areas of our lives. As an obvious example, an artist wouldn't get very far without having a source of inspiration. Taking that further though, the businessman in his office would enjoy his job far more if he had a little inspiration to flare up the work he's doing. Similarly, we incorporate the need for divine inspiration into our daily spiritual and magickal work. We know that spells are more effective when they're not cookie-cutter copies from a book. The reason being, when we work magick that's backed up by the spark of inspiration, we're aligning that magick with another source of divine power. And who couldn't use more power for their spells? In my experience, inspiration seems to be one of those things that sneaks up on you when you least expect it. It doesn't usually feel like it's around when you need it to be. I don't think I'm alone in that experience. Have you ever woken up in the middle of the night with some awesome idea, but were too tired to get up and jot it down in a notebook? How about a vision of the perfect ending to that short story you've been working on? It hits your brain when you're cruising down the interstate highway with no way to record it. Why does this phenomenon happen? I believe it's because we're more open to inspiration when our brains are in an alpha or delta state. When the brain is in an alpha state, its waves are operating at a frequency range of 8 - 12 Hz. Think of the times when you get lost in a great movie or book or when you're lost in deep thought sequences. When the brain is in this state, it's operating outside of the normal beta or "active state" that it's used to. This causes the brain to enter the perfect conditions required to enter a state of inspiration. Any seasoned magick worker knows how to enter these various states at will, whether they prefer to call them by their scientific names or not. Any time we enter into a ritual consciousness either through meditation or intentional movement, we're activating these non-beta states, opening ourselves to divine inspiration and possibility. This is part of the reason why ritual and meditation are so important. The Witch knows that when she's prepared to receive inspiration, she can use it in the most effective means available to her. We can channel, record and implement it when our non-ritual lives resume.

In ancient Greek thought, the muses were considered the central source of inspiration. Originally, three muses were said to make up the muse pantheon; Aoide the muse of song, Mneme the muse of memory and Melete the muse of practice. Later on their pantheon was tripled for each turning them into nine. The muse most interesting to me in the work that is of most concern to us right now is Melete, the muse of practice. In the beginning of this chapter we discussed the struggles that accompany regularly showing up for practice. Melete is the perfect muse to help you with this. The best way to call upon a muse is to speak the written word or better yet, to sing it.

Melete I call to thee
let my song be true,
when inspiration comes to me
I gift it back to you.
Melete I call to thee
by grace of moon and sun,
grant the things I wish to be
let this work be done.

If you're having a particularly hard time, try making an offering. The best offering to a muse would be to speak a poem or gift some sort of original artwork. Your own would be best, though speaking any classical poem with passion and intent would serve to please these gentle goddesses enough to pay you a visit. When they do stop by and you find yourself with a flare of inspiration, be sure to write it down and thank the muse you called upon.

Your relationship with the energy of inspiration will only be strengthened by working with them so it's a valuable thing to be on good terms with them.

The four winds and other air spirits

In deepening our relationship with air on the pentacle, it is essential to build positive relationships with the spirit allies that embody or occupy that element. Every culture has a vast array of spirits associated with each element, especially with the element of air due to its associations with the four winds of Greek mythology. These Greek winds were collectively called the Anemoi (*winds* in Greek). These mysterious spirits don't show up very frequently in Greek literature making their depictions harder to pinpoint. Some have said that they manifest simply as wind gusts and in no other form. In other references, they appear as winged men. Boreas the north wind, is most famously associated with this image. Wiccans will recognize references to the winds in the extended version of the Wiccan Rede.

> *When the wind blows from the east, expect the new and set the feast.*
> *When the wind blows from the south, love shall kiss thee on the mouth.*
> *When the wind blows from the west, departed souls shall have no rest.*
> *Heed the north wind's might gale, lock the door and drop the sail.*

Again, we see the north wind standing apart from the others in the first few words of its line. The north wind brings the storm and the temperature drops that frequently occur when the seasons are shifting from autumn to winter. The four winds can be easily honored when calling upon the guardians of the four directions which is common in many Witchcraft rituals. Some believe that these guardians embody the four winds anyway, without having to be called out apart. I tend to believe that the winds are their own unique spirits. When I call upon the directional guardians in ritual, I imagine that the winds from that direction are "blowing in" the energies I need from that direction. My directional guardian steps into place within the circle and a strong gust of directional wind follows. I often imagine that they're blowing in blessings to my space, or blowing out unwanted forces or situations when I'm in a state of cleansing. The next time you're in a ritual incorporating the four directions, try calling upon the spirits of the winds for aid and see what type of connection you can establish. There are many things the wind can teach us about the element of air and the changes it creates, inside and out.

What about faeries?

Faeries are wildly popular spirits associated with air. In some Witchcraft theologies, the fey are even considered to be the very embodiments of each element. No element is as closely associated with the fairy realm as is air. When most people think of a fairy, they think of the tiny winged sprites that dance from flower to flower, buzzing about like a hummingbird. In reality, these are just faeries of air or sylphs. The sylphs are known for creating the enchanting woodwind music of the forest. Legends in the old worlds of Europe abound about such music. Its voice reaching your ear could either confer great blessings or a terrible curse. As Witches, we seek only constructive relationships with these beings so there's no reason why we can't work with them to deepen our practice on all levels. Faeries are gatekeepers between the worlds. They constantly live in a state of consciousness that we often strive to be in when engaging in meditation or ritual. Many believe that the fair-folk are a race of demi-god creatures, not quite pure divinity, yet dancing on a higher vibration than the human race all at the same time. When we call on the faerie realm, we're inviting in the shamanic and ecstatic side of air. This type of air brings joy, laughter and every kind of merriment.

Think of the last big, deep, belly laugh you had. Laughter like that means you've been touched with the ecstasy of air. On occasion, we laugh so hard we feel like we can't breathe. Think about the last time you experienced a laugh like that. What brought it on? How long ago was that? What can you do to encourage your next full bellied laugh?

Exercise – Meeting the ecstatic air spirits

For this exercise, try to visit a place that gets nice big gusts of wind. Don't necessarily rely on a windy day but rather, a place that gets this sort of airy attention based solely on its location and structure. Wind gusts are physical manifestations of this normally invisible element. Experiencing the wind and learning to speak with it is the best way to develop a deeper relationship with the air spirits. One of the first "showy"magickal things I learned from a teacher as a child was communing with and directing the wind. Since wind energy is very responsive to summoning, the practice of wind calling can lend great confidence to your communal practice and helps to remind you that the spirits are watching. First, my teacher stood behind me and outstretched my arms wide. She told me to breathe inward as I pulled my arms back. On the exhale, she pushed my arms forward. We did this a few times trying to match the natural "breath" of the wind. Though wind doesn't really have a physical inhale/exhale process, it can sometimes feel like it. Try this exercise for a while and see if you can match up with the natural rhythm of the wind. Once you've got that down, try to change its rhythm with your movements and will. The point? Besides being just plain fun, we're taking part in a natural process. It is not "power over" anything, but rather "power with". I believe that physical manifestations of the elements enjoy interacting with us. If they didn't, it wouldn't feel so good when they do. A breeze on a summer day can feel almost life-saving. The warm sun kissing my face when I lay in the grass in the spring. These are all physical interactions with elemental beings. When I sway with the wind, I'm inviting the spirits of air to come play with me. Later on when there is more serious work to be done, the elemental remembers our time together. I also remember what it was like interacting with that element and so it will be easier down the road to re-connect when I need to.

It's all in the wording

You might be familiar with Scott Cunningham's famous "13 Goals of the Witch": Know yourself. Know your craft. Learn. Apply knowledge with wisdom. Achieve balance. Keep your words in good order. Keep your thoughts in good order. Celebrate life! Attune with the cycles of the earth. Breathe and eat correctly. Exercise the body. Meditate. Honor the God and Goddess With air, I'm particularly concerned about number seven, keep your words in good order. Because words are part of the DNA of communication and communication is governed by air, we must consider the words that leave our mouths as part of the work we contribute to the world, for good or ill. I'm not the most eloquent speaker, and I'll admit that I love a good coffee gossip. That's why for me, I need to be more mindful of what my words are doing. As I get older I learn that not all information needs to go directly from my brain and out of my mouth. I have choices here. I have the ability to think about the things I say and attempt to forecast how those words will change things down the road. Language, especially in magick, is quite an expansive subject. Whole volumes of lore are written about the importance of language and spoken word in religious and mystic practice. Though certain cultural traditions placed an emphasis on keeping lore oral, many cultures took great joy and art in the practice of writing things down to keep the wisdom alive. The concept of writing things down to preserve knowledge is obvious, but there is more subtle value to the magick worker. The act of writing and speaking is an act of magick in and of itself.

When we commit words to paper or verse, we're translating thought and energy into form and force. Writing and speaking aren't just acts of creativity, they're acts of creation.

Many magicians and witches favor systems of ancient writing and magick alphabets that are believed to lend power to prayers and spells. The idea is that the language itself carries a power, a force all its own. This extra power gives the magickal work a nice boost. In addition to the "omph" you get from the alphabetic symbols themselves, the concentration it takes to write in another language lends focus and will to your magick. We all know that magick performed with focus and will is more likely to come into fruition than spells that lack those things. I highly recommend to my students that they learn and become fluent in at least one form of a magick alphabet. Not only is it useful to know for spells, but it can lend a bit of secrecy to your workings and enable you to hide things like Book of Shadows or magickal journal entries if you need to. Plus, being able to say that you know another language is just really cool.

Here are some magickal alphabets common in modern neopagan practice.

Theban

Theban is also called the Honorian Alphabet and the Witches Alphabet. The alphabet was originally seen in 1518 and credited to Honorius of Thebes, who some believe is an entirely mythical character. Who then devised the Theban script? Why is it now so popularly used by witches as an alphabet? Not much is known to be honest. What we do know is that the egregore (remember that word?) built up around this alphabet through generations of magick workers is strong, tangible and legitimate. Using Theban as your magickal alphabet can help you connect with your "Witch Blood" and your hidden company of Pagan ancestors.

Futhark Runes

Runes have always been my favorite system to use as a form of writing. The runes are from the northern European peoples and were widely used in Germany, Sweden, Norway and Denmark around the first or second centuries AD. Though there is some debate as to their origins, language scholars contend that the first runes were probably derived from Old Italic letters, language from the Etruscans on the Italian peninsula. I was taught that the power of the runes are limited only by human imagination. Though I don't have a very strong affinity for Northern Traditional practice, the runes have always been a staple of my magickal practice, especially in writing. Some argue that because each rune is a unique powerful symbol, using the system as an alphabet can give you a messy "magickal alphabet soup". I prefer to work from experience and I've had nothing but good experiences in using the runes for everything from magick, divination to writing. Using the runes as a language symbolizes the sacrifice of time and patience that we give to magickal practice. Odin hung upon the great Tree of Life just to gain an understanding of the mystery of the runes. From this lore, we know that to get, we must give. To gain understanding, we must sometimes undergo trial.

Veit ec at ec hecc vindga meiði a netr allar nío, geiri vndaþr oc gefinn Oðni, sialfr sialfom mer, a þeim meiþi, er mangi veit, hvers hann af rótom renn. Við hleifi mic seldo ne viþ hornigi, nysta ec niþr, nam ec vp rvnar, opandi nam, fell ec aptr þaðan.   I know that I hung on a windy tree nine long nights, wounded with a spear, dedicated to Odin, myself to myself, on that tree of which no man knows from where its roots run. No bread did they give me nor a drink from a horn, downwards I peered; I took up the runes, screaming I took them, then I fell back from there.
- *Hávamál*, stanza 138

Ogham

Also known as the Celtic Tree Alphabet, Ogham is comprised of a series of notches and lines that run out of and through a singular vertical line. Ogham was originally used to write Old Irish around in the medieval times. The system first appeared in stone inscriptions around the same time as the elder runes. The reference to the alphabet as a "tree alphabet" comes from each symbolic letter being named after a sacred tree.

Much like the runes, many people use Ogham as a magickal and a divinatory system. They're best carved onto staves, small notches of wood, and placed into a bag or box for selection. I recommend using Ogham for writings or acts of magick that involve deep work with devas, faeries and other nature spirits. In our later work with Earth, we'll revisit working with trees and the nature of terrestrial beings.

Hieroglyphs

Hieroglyphic is a pictographic language so it's not actually accurate to use the characters as an alphabet like we think of today. Regardless, I know many people who do use the common alphabetic letter system and are quite happy with it. Again, do what feels right for you. It seems like it would be a time consuming task to draw each little picture as a letter but I can see it being helpful for attuning oneself to the ancient Egyptian deities and powers. Focus on their symbols written as prayers and spells could work wonders for Egyptian-themed workings. Followers of the Kemetic paths are more inclined to use this system. If thoughts are things (and indeed they are), then words exist in a harder form of reality than even our thoughts do. Think of a thought as the intention of the spell or magickal working. The thought comes from the source and is relatively formless. When we add our personal ideas, our doubts, hopes and other human emotions, all of those things add to the development of the thought form and decide how it will get formed into words.

The impact of this process is clear; every thought is a prayer, every word is a spell. Everything is magick and there is nothing that is not connected to the all. This hermetic "Principle of Mentalism" is true for all people, but especially the magick worker. We are attuned to forces that lend power, form and outcome to the things we do. We must be especially careful about the things we say. We must keep our words in good order so we can maintain our own order and the order of the immediate environment around us. This is why the prayer work we discussed earlier is so important. However, let's challenge ourselves to enact this wisdom outside of the circle where it really matters.

Air as gateway

Now that we've discussed the ways in which we can develop relationships with air, you have a hint as to how the other elements will be approached. When we learn things like the spirits, creatures, and values associated with each element, we develop a plan of action for establishing greater connection.

Similar themes will make themselves known within other elements. The most important thing to keep in mind is that you'll be drawn to do some work in certain areas more than others. This is perfectly natural. Development of mastery in any particular area is very helpful for the overall work as a whole. We start with air (in the air) as a way to bless the rest of our way moving forward.

Chapter 2

Fire

I am building a fire, and every day I train, I add more fuel.
At just the right moment, I light the match.
- Mia Hamm

Fire is civilization. When the humans of the Earth began to use and maintain concentrated forms of fire, they began to rise up into the era of cities and society. Being able to use fire gave people the ability to cook food and store it for later consumption. It allowed them to survive the harshest of winters. Because of this, you can imagine the very rich and detailed lore and mystic thoughts surrounding this vital element. In the cold seasons, families spent long lengths of time sitting around the hearth for warmth until the icy winds subsided. These family gatherings nurtured what we now think of as "oral tradition" - traditions of lore passed down via word of mouth from person to person. Stories were spun and great magick was born here. The fiery hearth, so vital to the well-being of our ancestors, is just as vital a resource to us, if we only open to its mysteries.

Will

I must say that even as someone with the sun in Leo, it took me quite a while to open myself to the mysteries of fire. I am still learning them. I suspect that my resistance comes from the length of time that I avoided my own power, knowing that it was ok for me to embrace it and make the changes I needed to make in my life. I ran from fire, I ran from my will. Will is a tricky subject, and yet one so central to all systems of magickal belief that it's impossible to avoid. Many of us try to avoid it anyway or at least get by on a mediocre understanding of it. Well what is it then? In short, will to me is a combination of desire and action. It's that tiny space where the two meet and decide between having movement or stasis. I can desire something for as long as I want to, but it means nothing unless I make the choice within myself to pursue it. This is when we learn that will is more than just a "thing" inside of us. It's a unique part of us that entirely comprises one of our "selves" all on its own. When our will is completely engaged, we tell the world around us that we're ready to claim success, know love, and live for all that we desire. If you've ever felt a nudge or a tingle that you needed to do something that you're already aware of, this is the voice of your will speaking to you. You might notice that the feeling is similar to one of those "tugs" from intuition. The difference? Most tugs from will come from the things you're already fully aware of. The will knows the scope of the situation. Intuition already did the work of gathering the information you needed. After you assembled the message that your intuition brought you, it's up to your will to make you get up and take the message into action. Aleister Crowley's religion of Thelema talks expansively about will. Indeed it is will that's a core tenet to their philosophy and core values.

Do what thou wilt Is the whole of the Law. Love is the Law, Love under Will. Love and compassion must be the Foundation of Will.
-Book of the Law

Will is sloppy without compassion. Though a genuine power can be raised out of anger, love and compassion are the building blocks of successful magick that lasts. The Witch who enacts her will out of love knows that once the seeds are planted and her will is set fourth into motion, she can let all the rest begin to fall into place. How then do we groom our will? Quite simply, showing up for daily practice (as discussed in the previous chapter) really seems to be the best place to start. Not only are we telling ourselves that we're doing something every day because it is our will to do so, but we're cultivating a strong magickal presence in the meantime. Cultivating a strong and healthy will allows you to build your skills in other areas which then strengthen your entire foundation. When the muscle of your will is growing and strong, you have the power to invite other helpful powers into your life to assist your goal of becoming a truly self-actualized human being. When I think of my biggest experience in cultivating will, I think of my training in basic meditation many years ago. I think that when we meditate for years, we forget how difficult it can be for some people to start out in the practice. When I started, I just could not focus on well, not focusing. The concept of clearing my mind or focusing on one thing at a time seemed so alien to me. My ego didn't like this, and it certainly let my will know that it wasn't happy. I knew that as a young witchling I needed to master this skill, although I didn't really want to. It was hard and I wanted to get to the spells. So onward I pushed and every day after I came home from school, I'd sit my butt on the floor and try different meditative practices. And you know what? It seemed to get easier every day. I say "seemed" to get easier because the challenge of the practice itself wasn't changing, it was me who was changing. In pushing up against the resistance of not wanting to meditate, my will was growing stronger. After a while, I could meditate for ten minutes, then for fifteen, then to twenty etc. My muscle grew and I was able to carry more "weight" (time) doing this practice effectively. Now, meditation ceases to be an issue because I've integrated it into my being and my will knows that I need it to do this work.

Spell to cultivate will

I like to think of the power of will as being ruled by Mars. Because of this, I recommend doing this exercise on a Tuesday which is ruled by that planet. I find that morning time at sunrise is a strong time to commit to acts of will. My morning devotional practice is what I use much of my will-strength for and so this time feeds into my goal of sustaining a successful daily practice. On a sheet of paper, write down something in your life that you could use more willpower for. It could be showing up to daily practice, sitting down to write that novel, anything. If you can't think of anything specific, you can simply write "cultivating a strong will".

Next, obtain a red candle which you'll use to petition the spirits of fire. If you can make the wording of your goal short enough, you might even be able to inscribe it right on the candle. Feel free to dress the candle with any appropriate herbs that bring inner strength and mental power. I recommend High John Root, Caraway, Eyebright, Horehound, Rosemary, Rue, Savory, Spearmint, Echinacea, Plantain or St. John's Wort.

Light the candle and fold up the sheet of paper, holding it tight in your hands. Focus on the flame of the candle. Feel the fire encircling the paper, the area around you, and your entire being. Say in a strong voice aloud:

> *Spirits of fire, stir without. Spirits of fire, stir within.*
> *Hear this call, this proclamation*
> *of strengthening and cultivation.*
> *Fire of will, arise and grow*
> *Witches flame, burn and glow*
> *I call my power, claim my will*
> *that this Great Work to be fulfilled.*

Set the paper alight and toss it into a fireproof container or a cauldron if you have one. If you have any herbs left over from the candle dressing, you can sprinkle them on the flames at this time. Stare into the flame and feel the fire of your true will burning away all within you that finds resistance at this time. Know that resistance is a natural part of life that you will never completely burn away. You're simply coming into communication and understanding with the resistance that's there. You might feel the need to repeat this spell regularly and that's certainly fine. I often include the above incantation in my morning devotionals as a way to recommit myself to my work and to my will. If you're someone who is already in possession of a healthy will, I encourage you to never give up the pursuit of making it stronger. Like any muscle, the will can become weak and limp if we don't work it out.

Embracing passion - valuing fire

Passion is one of the more obvious gifts that the Witch calls upon when invoking fire. But what is the true depth of passion? Where does it come from and how can we value it fully? Fire teaches compassion in degrees. It can be felt in its intensity on those oppressively hot August days. In its lower degree, it's felt when you bring your face closer to the flames of a candlelit altar. Like fire, balanced passion warms our lives and allows us the comfort of being in a place of safety and security. We talked about the power of the hearth and what it meant to the ancients. Spinning stories that stir our spirits or make our hearts jump, is passion. When passion is brought into life and magick, all the world becomes a dance. The expression "love what you do" comes to mind here. Though passion finds its birthplace in our second (belly) chakra, it usually finds its home resting within the depths of the heart. This isn't the only place it can live though. A person with a driving intellect might find that most of their passion is located within the front of their head. For the philosopher, it might be the back of the head. As an activist, I find that passion is usually resting around my throat chakra. I use my voice to express and nourish my passion. It matters where passion lives because when passion arises, either in anger or love, we know how to speak with it and ask it for help. To sense where your passion is, draw yourself into a meditative state. You might put on some music that makes you feel "passionate" or vibrant. You might wear clothing that makes you feel motivated or spray a fragrance that reminds you of your lover. As you sit with this, begin to think about what makes you passionate. What gets you out of bed every morning to complete the day? It's ok if it's not some strong noble endeavor. The monk might be passionate about sitting in silent prayer. The family man might be passionate about his children and spouse. Whatever it is, feel yourself surrounded by this energy and sense it rising from your belly chakra. It will probably manifest in the form of heat, or possibly a tingling sensation. Wherever it is, sense where it's going and where it comes to rest. Where does passion store itself within you? Once you know this, you'll be able to identify passionate reactions in your everyday life and call upon it when you need it, like within the throngs of an ecstatic ritual.

All's fair in love and witchcraft

Love. It's one of the most sought after forms of magick today. Chances are, when people know you're a Witch, they'll ask you about love magick at some time or another, even if they're just curious about it. This isn't surprising when you think about how love shapes most of our experiences and the way we view the world. People branded with the pain of love lost know its power. Some of the most famous charms and spells throughout history and literature were designed to draw forth the man or woman of one's dreams. We can all think of some classic methods whether real or fantastical. The traditional poppet, the charm bag and of course the potion. The tools and styles employed to work love magick are just as varied and diverse as the people using them.

With all of this fuss around the power of love, why is it one of the most controversial magickal subjects? I believe much of it has to do with people having some misguided ideas about love and where the magickal arts can be of help. The old adage "you must love yourself first before you can receive the love of another" says much about the issue. When we aren't open to love (or are open to a love of pain), there isn't room for much else to come in. Even those of us in happy and steady relationships will find that the true potential of their love for another is not met if they're not happy being with themselves. Though I won't claim to know much about the psychology or biology of love, I have a few observations from a magickal mindset on the biggest problems people face. Abuse - It's easy to enter into an abusive relationship when you don't have love for yourself. The idea that someone else has the power to make you happy and control the level of your love can create patterns that make it hard for us to break away from. At a time when I was in an abusive relationship, I spent a lot of time after I got out of it thinking about how I ended up there in the first place. I didn't really care about being happy and so I settled with what was there; an abusive jerk. It didn't matter that this person was harming me; all I knew was that it felt better than nothing. This is an illusion that's all too hard to see past. Once we see past it, we can begin to realize that loving ourselves means that we won't settle for anything less than being treated with kindness and respect by others.

Low Self-Esteem - Low self-esteem is low love. "I'm not pretty enough, I'll never be good enough at work to get a raise and I'll never be able to stand up to my mother-in-law." Having low love means that we lose the vision to see that everything we want to become is already within us. The potential for all of us to fulfill our Great Work and pursue our life's purpose is a seed that was planted deep within us from birth. We can nurture the seeds of potential with the fertile warmth and energy of love, of the divine fires within us.

Commitment - When we're not committed to living each moment from a place of love, how can we expect other people to put their commitments in us? If I don't do what I need to do by acting my spiritual practice every day, I move into each day with a state of disconnection from all my commitments. Other than making these simple changes in lifestyle, what more can we do to claim love as part of our right, as Witches to be balanced and happy? Magickal work would be the next obvious step. The love magick I describe here is much different than the love magick featured in the Valentines' Day editions of Cosmopolitan Magazine. The love magick I'll speak of here begins and ends with you. The resources that follow this passage will open the way to love and allow you to call back the fragile parts of your love that have seemingly been lost.

Ritual for calling back the soul of love

There is a common belief in many forms of Shamanism that throughout one's life, different parts of the soul can "chip off" and be lost due to traumatic and painful events. Proponents of these belief systems feel that the jarring emotional stress of things like losing a loved one, cause the lower parts of the soul to retreat as a method of self-preservation, to rejoin the body upon death. I'm not sure if I believe that actual parts of our soul are being fragmented and dispersed into the ether, but I do believe there to be a powerful truth in this.

Throughout our days we each expend a certain amount of energy doing any particular thing. If the thing we're doing is experiencing grief, depression or emergency states of fear, it's likely that those energies won't return to us unless we "call them home." Sure, we each regenerate our physical energy reserves by eating food and getting a good night's sleep, but what about our essence? The powers of our experiences. We know that any experience can be transformed and shaped into a tool of power and as Witches, it is our job to live in the highest level of power we can.

Once we realize this, we understand the importance of the practice called "soul retrieval" or "calling ourselves home." Though soul retrieval could really be used to call any part of you back, I feel that its use in calling love back is particularly useful.

How many times have we given up love to abuse, betrayal, jealousy, dishonesty and fear? How many times have other people projected those feelings onto us, dragging us into their state of disempowerment? My guess is that many people reading this will say "a lot." Imagine what we could do if we called back all of our love lost to heartache and distress. Imagine how much love we'd have left to give back, in positive ways, to the people around us we care about. This ritual will begin to help you do just that.

Before this ritual, I recommend taking a soothing shower or bath to relax and bring you into the right frame of mind. You might chose to add some loving scents to the water such as rose, ylang ylang or vanilla. You can use time in the tub as your pre-ritual meditation if you like.

When you're done with your cleansing bath, begin to set up your space. Be creative with this. Your soul parts will want familiar and appealing sights and scents to be drawn back. For me, I might lay a soft silky cloth over my altar and scatter jasmine and rose petals all about it. Red makes me think of love and jasmine has a "romantic" smell to me. We are romancing our own souls in a way. Think of things that you'd like a suitor to court you with. Court your own being into fullness.

Begin your ritual by dropping your awareness into your center point or your heart-center. For some, your natural center might be your heart anyway and that is a good place to work from for this purpose. If you have trouble finding center easily, begin by closing your eyes. See that dark "back of your eyes" vision that comes naturally when you shut your eyes. Little by little, allow your eyeballs to relax and go lower, bringing your awareness, your "mind's-eye" with them. Let your vision drop down to the bottom of the skull, down into the chest, and finally resting in the heart. Sense the physical heart pumping away, circulating rich, life-sustaining Witchblood. Rest with the feeling that everything in your body is emanating outwards from this point, and returning back to this point. Once you feel you've reached center, begin to enter a deep state of relaxation, and ultimately trance, in any way you favor. I like to tense and release each of my muscles starting with my head and working my way down to my toes. Don't forget to breathe throughout this process. Big and deep belly breaths that fill your entire diaphragm will help induce the state of trance needed for your work. I like to inhale for a count of seven, stay for a count of seven, exhale for a count of seven, stay for a count of seven and repeat. I've heard this called "the little death breath" because it has the ability to quickly get you into a state of trance rather easily with practice. Further "accessories" might help you achieve a deeper state such as ritual music. For workings like this, I prefer a steady and heavy drumbeat that mimics a slowly beating heart. Hearing a slow drum should automatically encourage your body to slow down and open up to this work.

Once you feel you're in a deep enough state of trance, bring your awareness back to your center heart. If your center is not your heart, begin again at the center and work your awareness slowly towards it. Don't rush the process. Proceed with a slow patience and make the process as easy on all your selves as possible. Now, touch your heart. Feel its soft and steady beat. Mimic the beat by gently taping your hand against your chest as you speak this statement of intention:

Heartsong, soulsong, my voice reaches out
Through minute, hour, day and year
Memory touching , around about
Speaking words my love to hear.
Return at once and make your haste
Back home to me who calls you near
We haven't got the time to waste
So trickle back and settle here.
Heart to heart and hand to hand

My love begins to heal
I mend you deep of rifts and pains
I call you back, and make you real.

As you can see, I prefer a rhyming structure because it helps me connect to the magick through poetic verse. If rhyming makes you feel silly or embarrassed, you could just as easily distort the words to make them not rhyme. Or better yet, craft your own statement of intention! It's your love you're calling back. You're reclaiming deep parts of yourself and it's important that you feel like you're creating a safe space for it to return to.

If you like, you can remain in a state of trance for as long as you need to. The state of trance when love is being drawn back to you can be a fantastic feeling. If you don't feel like you often have love covering you, then you might be compelled to lay there for longer than someone who does. This is fine. Remember though that you can come back to this place and back to this state at any time you like. Though the initial ritual can be as elaborate as you like, you'll find that performing it continually will be easier and easier. The process of reclaiming love can be a long one. I still call love back often. Take your time. When your work is done, be sure that you've grounded and centered. You can take in as much love as you need to but there's no need to overwhelm yourself. This energy can be intense. It's ok to let some of the extra drip down through grounding. Mother Earth can always use more love and she's always happy to take it.

Refinement - Fire in smithcraft and alchemy

The flame is a tool of refinement. Used well, it can burn away the unusual and unsightly. Used with integrity, it can burn away all the crud surrounding our outer shell. This is what happens in the forge. Think of the Witch in this case as the blacksmith of old. She sweats near the heat of the kiln fire, working away at the hard metals to make something useful. He strikes when the iron is hot, literally and figuratively. When we think of the power of smithcraft in the Pagan sense, we think immediately about the image of Brigit. Brigit, the Celtic daughter of Dagda is perhaps one of the most beloved of all Irish deities, and certainly beloved among all within the Celtic pantheon in general. Her powers are threefold: healing, poetry and smithcraft. In her role as Lady of the Forge, she wields the flame of the gods to make the armor of the spirit. Though the heat of her flame is intense, it is a healing flame. She tells us that by walking through the fire, we forge our destinies and light our pathways with passion and power. If only we dare. We already know that to will is the first step on our journey of fire. When we meet Brigit, we realize that we must dare to continue on. We must use the flame within us and the hammer in our hands. We strike the warm metal of our lives and bring about the tools of transformation. What within you is warm enough to bend? What within you is ready to be molded and made strong? Though the journey of forging our true being is always a work in progress, knowing what within us needs forging is a powerful milestone. Perform the ritual below to align yourself with the powers of the flame and the forge. Communing with the forge can soften our core so we can make it movable.

Ritual of the forge

Tools Needed
Oven-bake clay
Water
Flame (candle but you can also use a contained cauldron fire)
Hammer
Tool for inscription

Begin by forming sacred space in your usual manner. You might want to create a fiery setting of deep reds, blacks, and greys, the colors of the blacksmith. In your creation of space, it would be helpful to imagine yourself surrounded by the tools of the smith.

Your altar before you is the heavy iron anvil. All around you lay pieces of armor you're working on for your kingdom's warriors. Perhaps it's your own armor. The candles around you give off the heat of the intense kiln fire. You hear the clanking of the hammer against steel. You raise the hammer and invoke the Goddess of the forge.

Keeper of the forge, keeper of the flame
Brigit I invoke your name
Formed in earth and forged in fire
Wrought with force and pure desire
Warrior-poet I call you near
Move and stir and settle here.
Within the flames I seek my thrill
Join this space and forge my will.

Next, add water to the clay blessing both the water and the clay as you mix them together. The water here serves the function of fire in making the clay soft (as fire would with metal). Though the elements are different, the meaning is the same. As the clay churns through your fingers, pour your innermost divine image into the clay. What within you needs transforming? What within in you is in the process of transforming? Which parts of yourself need to come together in connection to make something new? As my teacher T. Thorn Coyle Says; "God Herself is in process."

You might even fold in some herbs or special water that holds power for you. I would add my totem plants that I feel represent my personality; lavender, lemon verbena and mandrake. A friend I have who has a knack for the Hoodoo arts would use Glory Water or Rose Water instead of plain water. The clay creation is somewhat of a poppet of your will. Let the correspondences you use represent what you use in your Great Work. Shape the clay into whatever shape you feel called to. If nothing comes to mind, shape it into a simple heart. If you want to get fancy you can form it in the image of the Venus of Willendorf, one of the first clay images of a Goddess ever discovered. You don't have to be a spectacular artist, but give it all you've got. If you were able to obtain a hammer, you can use that to beat out the curves of the image. In fact, I encourage you to do this, even if it's just in the kneading process. Connect with the process of striking the clay with the hammer. Feel what it would be like if you were beating the surface of hot steel from right out of the fire.

Once you have your little sculpture molded out to your ideal image, it's time to bless your work before firing it. For the blessing, just cup it within your hands and put it up to your face. Smell the organic materials of the formed earth. Feel the way the clay sticks to your hands or remains slippery from the blessed water. Infuse the sculpture with power, using your will to conse-crate it.

Heat up the oven based on the instructions of the clay brand you're using. Let this be a sacred act too. Once you set the temperature, sit by the oven and feel the warmth begin to radiate from within it. Meditate, sing a song, hum a chant, do something to further focus your intentions. Then, cook the sculpture. Continue with your focus work.

When your sculpture is ready, take it out and sit with your finished piece. Feel its heat. Let the warmth enter your skin and fill you with the power of the forge. Feel what it's like to touch the finished product of something that started with just an idea. Moving forward in your practice, you can set this atop your working space as a physical reminder of the Witches' power to bend, shape, and birth things into being.

Fire in alchemy

In alchemy, calcination is the first stage in the process of transfor-mation. A material is heated to the point of being reduced to ashes. Later on in the second stage of dissolution, the ashes are dissolved in water. Calcination is represented by sulfuric acid which affects all metals other than gold.

It's easy to see the connection here. We all experience times of calcination. It's a time of cleansing and it's usually not a walk in the park. It's hard, it burns, and it can feel like we're being burnt into nothing. And we can be. In the alchemy of the Witch, we purposefully burn away all that does not serve us. We burn away fear, shame, regret, dishonor and a whole host of other things that hold us back. Sometimes we enter the flames on purpose, knowing the things that need to be turned to ash. Other times, often when we least expect, we experience a "trial by fire". It's sink or swim here. The wise Witch knows that to swim is the only option. Better yet, we do the backstroke and swim to shore with grace and ease. When you enter the fire with dignity and bravery, we can control to some degree the parts of ourselves that need to be burned down. This isn't banishment, its invocation. We don't let our ashes blow away in the wind, they are a part of us and we need all our being to be fully powerful people. No, instead we gather up our ashes just when the gold of our inner being starts to shine through. Later when we're ready, we can dissolve the ashes of our refinement and continue to create. This is a sort of esoteric way of saying "what does not kill us, makes us stronger". Let's not kid ourselves now- no one likes to hear that. I most certainly don't. Accepting the truth of spiritual refinement as a tool for personal growth is an "inconvenient truth". It doesn't always feel helpful when we get messages like that, from any source. Think about it though, you can probably look back to many periods of strife that resulted in you emerging as a more vibrant person somewhere later down the road. It might show itself outwardly or inwardly depending on how you integrated the process. For our purposes, we want to integrate the fires of refinement into all of our beings. And you know what? Each time we do this, the hard parts about life can seem more and more manageable. It's not that we become used to it in a way; rather, we use the heat of fire to expand. When we expand, we make more room for possibility.

The next time you find yourself in an intense moment of personal strife, try uttering this prayer to expand your being outwards. Make room for better things to enter.

Sacred flame, fires of refinement
Take my burning tears, bless them with water
Take my knotted belly, cool it with earth
Take my gasping lungs, expand them with air
Take my brittle heart, warm it with the fire of spirit
I breathe this in, all of this
Nothing is beyond my flame, I burn with the all
I burn with the anger, the hurt, the dark night
I burn with these things and let them fill me
I ingest them, fill my warm belly
Fires of refinement, my spark ignites them
Sacred flame, fires of refinement
Dissolve, disperse, cleanse, return

Between each line, you can take a sharp intake of heated air. Each time you can expand your belly and exhale slowly. Each inward breath is bringing in fire. Each outward breath is pushing out the ash of what no longer serves you. The energy left inside, is gold.

Imagine what we would be like if we were able to immediately change any damaging thing that comes our way into something that can make us powerful and strong. Imagine if we didn't try to banish everything we didn't like, but invoked it and changed it. We would be very powerful beings. This is what personal alchemy does when we're dealing with fire.

Awakening to psychic insight

I know many people who would put psychic power in the category of water, ruling powers like intuition and "gut instinct". However, I feel that psychic ability strongly favors fire. Why?

Simply put, a person's psychic ability "lights up" the area around them. When we engage with our psychic self, it can often feel like someone is lighting a match within a dark room.

By psychic insight, I mean any sort of mental-based sensing ability beyond the five basic physical senses (although psychic experiences often manifest easily through the five). When the idea of placing importance on psychic power was presented to me as a Witch, I was confused about why. It seemed very separate from magick, in a way that was uninteresting to me. That was before I noticed how useful having those skills truly is. Developing psychic insight is important to the well-trained Witch for several reasons:

1) It's useful in healing practices where we need to sense out an illness or problem area
2) Sensing energy well is a key component to performing successful magick
3) Insight to our past helps us build a stable foundation in spiritual practice
4) Insight to our present helps us remain "in the moment" and keep us centered
5) Insight into our future helps us determine what course of action to take in the present
6) Increase in psychic power affects all the energy bodies, not just the psychic self

This list could easily fill pages. The point is, growing psychic power isn't just about seeing the future and picking up random impressions from people and places. Having psychic ability adds a clarity and focus to your magick.

The process of increasing psychic skill can seem daunting to people. I very much resisted this part of my craft for a long time. I thought it meant long hours of trance work, divinations, and arduous intuitive exercises. However, the meat of psychic skill is gained through dedicated meditative practice (which we covered early on). Meditation stills busy minds and engages the divine (psychic) mind. If you already maintain a daily meditation practice to some extent, you're half way there! You don't need to just sit around and wait for your psychic skills to grow on their own though. Through different exercises and workings, you can speed up the process just a little bit. Though there is no substitute for dedicated meditation work in the spirit world, you can use the workings that follow to supplement your psychic growth.

Psychic tea

Brew a batch of this tea add a splash of it to your beverages throughout the course of seven days. It's ok to make it strong since you'll be diluting it within other drinks.

2 parts Chamomile
1 part Anise
1 mugwort
1 part lemongrass

Psychic incense

Burn small portions of this blend each night before bed. The fumes will charge the air with psychic power that will soak into your consciousness during your dream time. This is a great mixture to burn while you drink your psychic tea.

1 part Wormwood
1 part Eyebright
1 part Rose (petals)

Opening the third eye

There is a period of time in the morning that we experience if we're not immediately jolted out of bed (like say - by an alarm clock) where we regain waking consciousness right before we open our eyes. We're in a period of sleep and waking. The body is resisting movement because it's emerging from its most relaxed state and so the physical senses are slightly dull. Use this time to open the third eye.

When you find that you're awake but have not yet fully opened your eyes, feel your third eye, that space on your skull between your two physical eyes, opening up. You might imagine rays of light like a sunrise creeping out of the opening. You might imagine it's an actual etheric eye, seeing out into all places and times. As strange as it might feel, open your third eye fully. Blink with it. Look in all directions. With your physical eyes still closed, what do you see with your mind's eye? Take mental notes and record them once you're up and getting ready for the day. Continued practice with this will help you open the third eye at other times of the day.

Psychic record keeping

As you move forward with your work on increasing psychic presence, you'll want to record your impressions in your magickal journal or book of shadows. You might keep a separate dream journal for this, but I find it useful to record all impressions, including dreams, in one place. When I wrap up my work week, I can run through all my recorded impressions and take note of occurrences that took place within the frame of my life. In a way, simply being aware of this will increase our psychic insight in its own right.

As any good Witch knows, having a strong psychic foundation will bring resilience and flexibility to your magick in ways that it otherwise couldn't. Honing the third eye can even keep you from needing to perform certain types of magick in the first place.

Creatures of fire

The spirits who live of the flame are both fantastic and frightening. On one hand, we have the salamander which is seen as a direct manifestation of fire itself. On the other hand we have creatures like the medieval dragon that uses fire to express their sometimes fearsome temperament. The creatures of fire teach us about ordeals and the bravery required to experience them. Most spirits of fire should be approached with caution, for to misunderstand their nature could lead to a good burning!

The Salamander

We first see mention of the mysterious salamander in 23 AD when Pliny described them as *"an animal like a lizard in shape and with a body starred all over; it never comes out except during heavy showers and disappears the moment the weather becomes clear."* Of course, these traits are consistent with the actual salamander amphibian. This can cause confusion until you consider that Pliny actually did make a distinction between this creature, and the animal (which was back then classified as a lizard). Pliny along with Aristotle both attributed the salamander with the power to defend against and extinguish fire, although some skepticism existed.

The salamander is said to appear completely surrounded by flames. In the plain sense, this would probably be explained by early writings about animal salamanders which made their habitats within hollowed logs. When the log was placed within the hearth, the salamander would appear to mysteriously emerge from the flames.

Based on its form (being surrounded by flames) the salamander can represent adaptation. Much like the alchemical process, the salamander can be seen as a creature of both myth and science, walking between the world of form and spirit whenever it sees fit. I believe the salamander is a symbol of the lowest vibration of fire, primal and ancient.

We can call upon and invoke salamander energy when we need intense bursts of fire to flow into our lives. You can imagine yourself resting in a deep cave, safely tucked away from the cares of the world. Yet slowly, your energy becomes warmer. The risk you take by being visible sparks the flame within you. Fire circles around you but you feel no pain. The flame becomes part of your own biology as you dance in heat and ecstasy with the mighty elementals.

The Phoenix

The phoenix can be found in abundance in many cultures including the Greeks, Egyptians, Russians and Persians. Though cultural context has a unique spin on this bird-creature, the form of a flaming bird is always the constant. Though not in flame-form at all times, the phoenix is said to burst into a brilliant spectacle of flame and is reduced to ash when it reaches the end of its life cycle. After a time, a new bird is born out of the ashes.

The alchemical symbolism is very easy to see here. When phoenix burns up, she enters the stage of calcination, inciner-ating all that she is. The reemerging from his ashes is the end stage of dissolution when something new is born out of the wreckage. There is debate about whether the phoenix is an immortal bird, continually re-birthing itself over and over. Some believe that the ash bares the offspring of the bird before it. In observing what its cycle means, this really doesn't matter. What matters is that something new comes from something old. There is power in what we seemingly "leave behind" when we shed our skin for a new form. The phoenix shows us that through the lessons of the flame, we should not fear death or really any ending. The end of a process brings only opportunity for newness.

Rather than being directly invoked as an elemental, I find it helpful to simply observe each stage in our lives as reflecting the states of the phoenix. Sometimes I am in my unassuming "normal" form. I do my work and live my life unnoticed by the eyes of those who aren't paying attention. Other times, I flare up and ascend to the heavens in a magnificent show for all to see. Still sometimes, I burn out, return to ash, and make my rest. What Phoenix-stage are you in at this moment? How about this week, or this year? Being observant of this can help you predict patterns of what's to come.

Djinn (Genies)

You might be surprised to find djinn (genies) under the category of fire. In doing research for this work, I always thought of them as creatures of air. I admit this was a mistake based on my pop-culture preconceptions of what they might look like when fully manifested in physical form. Instead, the djinn are described in the Qur'an as made of "scorching fire" (Qur'an 15:27).

It might also surprise you to know that these genies aren't often humanoid in form. In most of the ancient literature describing them (both Islamic and pre-Islamic) there are different types of djinn, each being able to attain any number of forms. They are also known to take human form, though in these rare instances it is usually not to the benefit of another human and more often for some kind of nefarious purpose.

The idea of genies being bound by the wishes of humans probably comes from the legends of King Solomon who was said to have employed any number of genies for various tasks according to his will. The passages referencing this also indicate that these spirits were released upon his death. This leads me to believe that the djinn generally have their own will, although they may be controlled by some type of sorcery.

I really don't think it useful or wise to call upon an unstable type of spirit such as the djinn. I list them here because like the fire creatures listed before them, we can learn from their existence. The djinn show us that fire is truly an untamable element. Though the djinn may be subject to rule by certain external forces, they are a primal shadow force that live off their own interests.

The "genie" however, I think can be called upon to benefit. This is where etymology confuses us. I place djinn and genie together because their names were born of the same sound. Although there are many similarities, genie is latin-based and is a reference to one's "genius" or personal shining body, Holy Guardian Angel, etc. In this use of the name, the genie is said to be assigned to each person born to earth, much like a pre-selected spirit guide that most are familiar with. With this association, it's reasonable to say that one might call upon their genie/genius to connect them to their higher self or with their Great Work. When in doubt, work within a protective circle and listen to the voice of the soul.

Blood

Blood in any cultural context (Witchcraft especially) is quite the controversial topic. When asked about blood in any way, many public Witches will put on a shocked face and exuberantly proclaim that Witchcraft does not use blood in ritual or for any means. Such a thing would be just dark and barbaric, right?

In all my research, I never really came to a conclusion on why blood is such a taboo topic in the Craft. I realize the concept of sacrifice and death is something that many Pagans like to avoid talk of when working with the public, but what about within our own circles? Why has blood become a taboo among many of our own traditions? These are the questions you should ask yourself when you think about blood and if/how you want to use it in practice. I consider blood to be ruled by fire because it is blood that keeps us warm. When we die and our bodies cease to pump blood, we become cold, inside and out. Blood pumps faster when our bodies heat up in exercise or sex. The phrase of putting our "blood, sweat and tears" into something is an expression of effort and will, both powers of fire. The core use of blood in my practice is in meditation. When I enter my still place in my core, I listen and observe my heart and the blood pumping through it.

Is it quick or slow? Does my blood need more iron or other nutrients? Performing a "psychic scan" of your blood can help you determine things like stress levels and the depth required to slow down and enter a lower state of consciousness.

Still, others use blood as a substance to fuel great magickal work. It has been said by many Witches that our "Witch Blood" is the most powerful tool we have and that we should use it externally if we can. I find both truth and disagreement with this. In truth, blood (like any organic part of us) is a powerful material. Magick workers have been using it for thousands of years and it may have been one of the oldest magickal ingredients in use on the planet.

Supporters of using one's own blood say that bringing something like that from your insides out into the air is a powerful symbol for the greater meaning of your work. They might also say that what you need to do to obtain your blood (usually a small pin prick or finger cut) is a great gesture of sacrifice to the gods. It tells them you risk pain for deeper mystery.

On the other hand, there are practical concerns here. Drawing your own blood - even a drop - risks infection and sickness. For this reason, I would advise against the use of blood in any group or partner setting. There are just too many ways it could go wrong.

Instead, you might want to work with blood on the inner planes. When I am doing deep magickal work, I sometimes call upon my Witch blood and the blood of my ancestors and the Mighty Dead who came before me to fuel my work. Though we may not have trinkets to use to connect with our ancestors hundreds of years in the past, we will always have our blood. Those before us live on in the blood, and their power does too.

Ego

Everyone has strong opinions on ego. Usually they aren't very positive. In the Eastern traditions, ego is seen as something the practitioner should drive to move away from, to "transcend out of." Because of this, ego is often demonized, sometimes to the point of being thought of as evil with no benefit to the spiritually-inclined person.

This idea of ego being made of pure malevolence has no place in Witchcraft. Many traditions of the Craft see the ego as one out of many parts of the self. Some might even say that the ego is its own self altogether. Regardless, it's not the monster hiding under our proverbial bed as we usually think. Can ego turn negative? Of course it can, just like any other part of the self can. The difference is always within the choice of the Witch and her relationship with it.

We all know what ego looks like in its negative form. It's the part of us that exemplifies detachment. It says "me first, you later." When we are in an unbalanced relationship with ego, we have a tendency to think that we're the only thing in the universe. This is because the ego is ruled by the sun, and the fire from it. The sun is the center of our solar system, but it is not the center of all things. When ego imbalance occurs, we lose sight of this and crave the attention that we think is rightfully ours. I have a strong inner Leo personality and I will admit I have to check myself and remind myself of this. Sometimes when I'm off balance with ego, I "check in" with it and figure out where the problem is. Usually it just means I need more time in silent sitting practice, to let my mind take back seat to my higher self. When the higher self is involved, you usually don't have to worry about ego imbalance as much.

When we're in positive relationship with ego, we are able to step back from overwhelming situations and come back to center in a way that is healthy. I am a firm believer that we should not "banish" the ego, but come into good relationship with it for this very reason. The leader who has a good strong ego has the ability to say no. He can recognize that he doesn't have to be involved with every aspect of a project. She can delegate tasks to other people with the trust that they'll be fulfilled in a way that's successful to the project.

Many of us know that person who we describe as having a "strong personality" but in a good way. This is the person who knows what they want, but uses their own Will to accomplish things and isn't interested in treading over others in the process. The person who is in a good ego balance can accept constructive criticism. They can recognize when something they aren't doing isn't working and passes it on to another person or stops it completely. A person in a good balance with ego is firm, yet flexible. They are strong, yet questioning.

Exercise - Evaluating ego

For this exercise, enter a light meditative state. Do some breath work that brings you into a gentle state of relaxation, but don't "trance out." The ego is a part of our physical and mental being so if we are to converse with it, we need to be in our bodies to some degree.

The next time you are in your gentle state of relaxation, shift your awareness to the center of your head, or even the brain if you can imagine it. With your will, ask to speak to your ego self. It probably has a lot to say so be sure to ask it this very specific question: "yes or no, am I in good balance with my ego." Await a response; it most likely won't take long.

If the answer is no, ask more questions. Ask why you are not in balance. Do you have over-ego or under-ego? Don't spend too much time thinking about specific instances; just let the light of your being answer these questions for you. If specific instances arise, your higher self is using these as an example. Make a mental note to return to them later. You might want to record this in your book of shadows or magickal journal so you can keep taps on your progress.

Developing a healthy relationship with ego is so important to the Witch. Not just by how it can endanger us, but how it can gift us. When we know who we are and what we need to do, strength emerges and we have the energy needed to open to possibility.

Chapter 3

Water

All water has a perfect memory and is forever trying to get back to where it was.
- Toni Morrison

There is much lore about water being the heart and origin of the human species. Many (myself included) would take that even further to define it as the source of ALL things, at least in the physical. It is said that the first creatures on the planet arose from the primordial womb of the oceans. Because of this, water is seen as our true ancestral home while on Earth.

Nothing can live on this planet without water. It is truly the stuff of survival. Just as wars have been fought over land and gold, so too has blood been shed over water and who controls it. The world's water supply is deeply in danger. The oceans are being devastated by pollution and over fishing. The rivers are becoming unsafe to drink from without a filtration system. And still, all too many have little access to water at all, paying high prices for just enough to keep them alive. We often take this for granted in the west, failing to appreciate water's true value, in both matter and spirit.

When we connect with water, we connect with what it means to be alive on the planet. We connect with what we have in common with so many countless species of animals and plants. Water is emotion, intuition, and the power of dreams. Come into relationship with water and all these gifts will be yours to hold.

Water: Void of the physical world

You may think of a void as nothingness, and I am inclined to agree. Except, the laws of energy teach us that energy cannot be created nor destroyed. What we think of as the "final frontier" of all things, is to some being, just the beginning. We can think of the ocean this way. Far less of the world's oceans have been explored than the earth's land masses. Each year scientists discover a vast array of fascinating (and often creepy) creatures that dwell in the watery depths below.

The point here is that just when we think we have come up against territory that seems as though it's a meaningless void, there is always more to explore. There are painful and beautiful mysteries hidden in the waters. And there is risk in exploring them. We risk the unknown, for each of us in our journey is exploring a place where "no man has gone before."

Water teaches us that there is power in pursuing the unexplored. Areas of the craft that touch upon things like dreams, shadows, and heartbreak are all considered "watery." Why? The parts of us that are watery are also lunar. For the moon pulls the shift of the tides and so too does it pull at the water within us. The moon demands a curiosity for what lies hidden below. Like the pull of the moon on the tides, it nudges you onward, to the most frightening and glorious reaches of infinity.

Japanese author Dr. Masaru Emoto was made famous when he performed a series of experiments on water claiming that human consciousness could affect the formation of its crystalline patterns. The basic frozen image of the water displayed a plain hexagonal pattern with no particularly interesting features. Emoto showed that projecting positive energies like "love" into the water resulted in beautiful and intricate patterns in its structure. On the flip side, projecting awful thoughts into the water such as "hate" and "fear" showed the crystalline patterns breaking apart and becoming distorted. If thoughts can effect water in this way, imagine how our constant thoughts affect the huge amount of water our bodies are comprised of. Are we constantly poisoning our water, or improving it? Though Dr. Emoto's work is up for debate and criticism, it does get us thinking about the possibilities of thought on water and other elements.

When we explore the watery power of the hidden, we open ourselves to more strength. The Witch with a curiosity for the mysterious is a Witch who is stepping into a receptive state. She is open to receive more than she previously thought she could carry within a limited worldview. Water only has shape when we form a container for it. With water, we can grow the containers of our souls. We can make for ourselves a cup that is truly never empty.

Meditation: Water as the void

Assume a comfortable position suitable for deep meditative work. For this meditation, I usually prefer to lie down on my back, facing up. To help your journey, you might put on some ocean sounds or even theta frequency tones (which mirror deep sea vibrations.) Put on some incense corresponding to your favorite watery plants. Herbs that are favorable to Neptune would be a good choice here.

Enter a meditative state as you normally would, with the intention of going quite deep. We want to eventually reach a trance-like state as the vehicle for our meditation.

In your mind's eye, see yourself surrounded by the black emptiness of the void. This is the space that existed before space. Before the power of the gods was organized into bodies of being. Exist within the peace of the nothing. As thoughts enter your mind, let them drift by like a cloud in the sky.

Soon, something tangible begins to form. The void around you starts to ripple. Is it becoming liquid? Or was it always liquid? Colors start to form out of the black. Darkness fades into hues of dark blue of all variations. You find that an ocean is forming all around and you are within its deepest caverns.

Tiny particles, usually invisible to the human eye, float around you. As if time were speeding up thousands of years per second, you can see sparks of electricity animate the particles as they change shape and grow. The particles become larger, glowing with life as they shape and arrange themselves into beings. Primordial animals of all kinds move about within your darkened field of vision.

Other than the creatures forming, you notice land forming all around you. You look down and see solid earth rising to meet your floating feet. It touches and begins to lift you up. The waters are flowing forcefully past your skin as you ascend. It thrusts you into a new world, the earth stretches up and out of the inky waters and into a cool dark air.

You look around and see the beginnings of the earth. All things begin to creep out of the watery depths, lined with the silvery light of creation, the gods guiding the progress of their births.

Take in the sights and sounds around you. What does it feel like to reach back into the beginning? What power exists within this place? Take as long as you need to discover it. Let it form enough so you might take it back with you.

When you're ready, see the modern earth springing up around you. Night gives way to day and four walls grow up around you forming the familiar space you find yourself in.

When ready, breathe into your physical body and come out of meditation. Record the images and your experiences in your journal.

Witchcraft and emotion

What role does emotion have to play in the art of the Witch? This widely debated question is one that is difficult for anyone to agree upon. The one thing that most of us agree on is that its role is an important one, whatever it may be. Emotion is an important vehicle for the will. Will, as we know, is part of the driving force for spell work and spiritual connection. Emotion is the motivation that awakens our will from its slumber. If will is a lock, emotion would be the skeleton key. The doors that it opens are often unknown.

My first teacher believed that one should never do magick when one is angry or upset. The energy is too sporadic and untamed, she said. There is truth to this, but there's also much more to the story. The energy raised in anger and strife is raised far quicker than energy raised in joy (most of the time.) The reason we usually stay away from raising intentional power in anger is that the anger is thought to color the power with that negativity. This can be the case, but it doesn't have to be.

What if anger and upset were simply the doorways to get us to enter places of power within ourselves? Anger and extreme sadness only have to get us there, they don't have to keep us there. Once we get to the height of power, we can use our will to transform the power into whatever we need it to be. We can ditch anger at the door when it no longer serves us.

With all things, this requires patience, practice, and a strong will. Can you work powerful protective magick in anger without allowing it to become a curse? Of course you can. Will you sometimes mess up in the process? Probably. But Witchcraft is as much an art as it is a science. Think of this as another thing to practice and perfect in your craft.

Eventually, we can enter states of powerful joy whenever we want and use that to fuel all our workings. Wouldn't that be nice? It's possible, though not easily achieved. The Witch who is in relationship with her emotions is a Witch you want to work with and learn from. This extends into mundane matters as well. The craft makes us all emotional, especially when we first start out. We tap into feelings that were previously buried deep, that we never thought we'd have to deal with again. Touching these deep places can flip our whole world upside down emotionally and can leave us feeling unbalanced and easily aggravated. When we figure out what each emotion means and what stands behind it, we achieve mastery with yet another important part of our selves. What if you could fuel everything you do in life (magickal and not) with joy rather than grief? What a beautiful world that would be.

Exercise - Showering with emotion ritual

This simple rite can be performed any time you have the ability to take a shower of any normal length. You can do this just once, or every day if you like. We do this ritual to remind us of how helpful it is to maintain a balanced sense of emotion, rather than living from one extreme to the next. When you associate different senses of feelings to these very physical experiences, you might remember when it's time to bring emotion into check, into a state of mindfulness.

Begin by stepping into the shower water at a temperature appropriate to your usual comfort level. Try to keep it as much on the medium side as possible. Once you're in, enter a quick meditative state and experience the joy of being under running water at a comfortable temperature. As you stand within this "medium gauge" think about how you feel when you're emotionally balanced. How does your mind feel? How does your spirit feel? Recognize how it's easier for you to think about and experience other things while existing within a naturally comfortable current.

Now, turn the faucet to hot, as hot as you think you'll be able to handle for a couple of minutes. Of course you don't want to scald yourself, but make it hot to just beyond the level of normal comfort for a hot shower. As you do this, feel yourself overwhelmed with either extreme anger or extreme joy (like in a caffeine rush). What are the benefits to this feeling? What are the draw backs? What does it feel like to exist within this "hot and bothered" state?

Turn the faucet back to medium and take your mind back within that balanced state. The extreme moods are brought into check as you're able to think with a rational mind and a pure heart. What does this change feel like? The rage or extreme joy probably feels a little less important than it did before. Remember the feeling of transition. To help you remember, you might even establish a mudra (hand signal) that you can use in your normal day. You can use this magickal "trigger" to help you transition to a "medium temperature" state.

Next, turn the faucet to extreme cold, as cold as you can stand it. In your mind, think of a time when you felt physically and emotionally drained. From either apathetic, to totally and utterly depressed. Notice how being this far away from the extreme heat is uncomfortable, but also makes you feel a little safer. You're not in any danger of being burned, but it's also not the most comfortable experience either. You can't take being in this temperature any longer than the hot side, even though the feeling is a little different. Does being in the cold make you yearn for medium temperature, or for the heat? Note this for later recording in your journal.

When you can't take the cold (or have somewhat adjusted physically), turn the faucet once more back to medium temperature. Notice how it feels to go from a place of emotional bleakness, to a place that's a little warmer. Feel what it's like to bring the fire back into your water. To a place that is neither flaming hot, or icy cold. Do you appreciate this balance more? Notice how after experiencing this wide range of temperature, you have a better sense of what you're comfortable with. This speaks to the value of feeling all things. It's important to feel anger when it comes along, and it's ok to experience the icy grip of grief when we need to as well. But to exist in happiness in the long term, we need to always come back to center. We need to touch upon the extremes in order to find our way back to the middle.

Followers of the western occult traditions will recognize this from the pillars of kabbalistic thought. Between the pillars of mercy and severity dwells the pillar of mildness. The kabbalist knows there is power in each pillar, but also that the most direct path to the divine is through the middle path. In fact, the shower ritual could even be used in conjunction with the middle pillar ritual itself.

Emotion into action - showing gratitude

Many Witches who sustain a deep regular practice consider gratitude a regular part of both their spiritual and mundane work. Gratitude means you're "thankful" obviously, but etymology tells us that it also means "good will." There's that word will again. Gratitude means not only being thankful, but having good will. They must both go hand in hand. Being thankful is wonderful, but putting your money where your mouth is by also having good will is where it really counts. Remember: a Witch's word is as good as his deed. When we summon positive emotion in our spiritual lives, it must also follow in the physical.

What does invoking gratitude do? For one thing, it makes us more observant of the blessings that are already present in our lives. When we take stock of all the things we are glad for on a regular basis, we start to have more to be thankful for. This energy is reciprocal and must follow itself. Second, being grateful when times are good helps bring me at ease when times are not so good. Sure, when I have an incredibly trying day my first thought isn't to look up into the sky and yell "thank you Goddess, for this horribly day, I am glad for it!" That wouldn't be sincere and my gods would know it. Instead, I can pad the bad with things that are good, by noticing the things around me that still tend to aid my success, rather than pull me down.

We must be active participants in this of course. We can't pick and choose when we have gratitude and what we want to apply it to. When I open up to gratitude for even the most mediocre of days, I'm telling nature that I love and accept it for everything that it is and is not. And in return, nature shows me the same respect. The spirits bring to us what we ask of them. Focusing on the "lack of" and the "could be but wasn't", will only bring more need and keep success away. I want to live within the full potential of my success at all times. I don't have time to want for things or to have a lack. To manifest my work in the world, I want to be fully equipped to serve my family, my coven, and my gods. Gratitude helps me do all this and more.

Exercise - The waters of gratitude ritual

This simple rite is well performed under the glowing light of a big, bright, full moon. To connect you with the powers of water further, you could even perform this in the planetary hour of a water planet.

For prep, gather petals from your favorite flower. Preferably they would be fresh, but dried petals will do if needed. Next, fill up a bowl with clear water. For this rite, it would be extra nice if the bowl were see-through, so non-colored glass would be best. The bigger the bowl, the better.

Gaze into the bowl softly and fall into a meditative state as best as you can with your eyes open. If you have trouble getting into a relaxed state with your eyes open, consider this a good time to start practicing. A Witch who is always at the ready can perform rituals with eyes open or closed.

As your gaze becomes softer, mentally set your intention to generate visions of all that you feel grateful for. This can be gratitude for that particular day, or for your entire life span. It can be about small things like a warm meal for lunch, or large things like the kiss of the morning dew as it brushed against your legs in the morning on the way to work. Whatever it is, let it fill your field of vision, and in doing so, fill the depths of the bowl. You might even run your finger across the water, creating ripples to signal the formation of a new gratitude thought. As you do this, you might say a prayer such as this:

By the living waters of the gods,
I ripple and vibrate with thoughts of gratitude
gratitude from my heart, and gratitude from my mind
let all that I encounter be encompassed by the spirit of gratitude.

When no more visions come to mind, sprinkle in the petals of the flowers. The petals from your favorite flowers represent the beauty in being thankful for all that was, all that is, and all that ever shall be.

I like to do this in a slow, mindful way by adding each petal slowly and letting it sail softly across the surface of the water. In this process, you can once again say a verse, this time invoking the beauty of gratitude:

By the living flower of the Queen of Nature
I ripple and vibrate with thoughts of beauty
beauty in gratitude, and beauty in love
let the flower of blessings bloom deep within my soul

Sit there for as long as you need, continuing to gaze within the bowl and upon the flower petals. Play with the petals and have them glide across the surface of the water. Notice how this is what it looks like when beauty collides with gratitude. Ripples form across the surface, and nothing remains the same.

You can perform the Waters of Gratitude ritual as frequently or infrequently as you like. Expressing gratitude (or simply being aware of it) doesn't always require a full rite. Living in the moment and being aware of the gold that surrounds us is the simplest and best form of gratitude we can give. Paying that gold forward is even better.

Thoughts on love

The love we feel for ourselves and others really is more than just any one emotion. Water rules love because it is the substance that nurtures and sustains all things. If it forms a symbiotic relationship with what it nurtures this ensures that what it's nurturing leads a successful existence.

Where love is concerned, magical ethics and theory get dicey. If ever there were a controversial topic in the art of witchcraft, it would be love. You've heard the horror stories – love spells going awry, cats falling in love with people, violent stalkers peering through windows et cetera. I must admit I believed a lot of this myself for a long time. As I get older and experience how magick works first hand, I really don't think love magick is anything to be concerned about in and of itself. Any magick has the potential to go awry if we dont know what we're doing or why we're doing it. Yes, love magick has a bad reputation in the magickal arts. Combine that with the spell-begger stigma (most spells people ask for by non-magick folk tend to be about love), and you get a hot soup of controversy.

Having falling in and out of love a few times in my life (I'll refrain from stating how many exactly), I've come to realize that like power in general, it is how you direct and use it that matters. In the hands of the ill-intentioned or inexperienced, it could at the least not work at all, and at the worst have some inconvenient side effects.

I think love is an important thing to consider when working magick. If we can't use magick to help with our love lives here in the physical world, then why would it be so extraordinarily cautioned? Surely it must work to some degree. To that I can give testament.

I truly believe that all effective magick stems from love. Even malicious magick can often find its roots in love...usually misused love for the self that is wasted. Love magick has been described as popping open a big river dam. The waters come rushing in and though it has a path to follow- it is somewhat unknown what will happen when the rapids begin to stir. To me, there is nothing more fascinating in magick than watching a working for love manifest. We call out to the spirits to make it so and they set out to find someone who will suit us for that time.

The other way that love rules water is around ice. This is the hard part about love. Sometimes our love can become stale and bitter to the point of freezing over. To the person who has this experience too many times, they can develop what many people call "a heart of ice." They become "cold hearted." What happens then is that the waters they once held are still there, only now they don't have the opportunity to flow. Stagnation never helps us. Water and love are only productive when there is a flow, an exchange. Without movement, there is certain death.

What can water teach us about love? The next time you commune with the water, ask it questions about someone you love. Perhaps you can even perform a scrying on this (a topic we'll explore shortly). When it comes to the emotional side of love, water will be the most effective element to consult. When we are in right relationship with water, the emotional side of our love lives will probably make more sense, just like our emotions in general.

If you plan to embark on a love magick plan in the future, consider your relationship to water before the working. Do you feel well connected to this element? When was the last time you communed with the creatures of water or acknowledged their existence at all? Engaging the spirits of water can help you chart a clear path in your journey of love. It may be a wild ride, but I really think it's worth the risk.

The Creatures of water

Beings who dwell in and around the watery depths teach us all things that our usual lessons about water teach, but they also show us how to embody those lessons in our daily Work. The creatures of water are both mysterious and fearsome, for we do not always know what lies beneath the depths, especially when the water runs fast or deep. They teach us about the risk inherent within all beautiful things. They ask us to take up the cup of sustenance and to drink deep.

Mermaids and Mermen

The idea of merpeople has always fascinated me, and not because "The Little Mermaid" was my favorite movie as a kid. I was the type of kid who my mother says "lived in the water" so the idea of being something that made its home in the water but still had humanoid features was just plain cool.

Popular culture glamorizes merpeople everywhere we look. Mermaids are almost always beautiful seductresses who rise up out of the water to exchange a kiss (or a little more) with unsuspecting male travelers passing by a watery source.

Mermaids show up in literature as early as 1,000 BC and have enjoyed a prime spot in the lore of many countries. Throughout that time, the image of sea-dwelling beings has been portrayed in every light from charming and fantastic to outright terrifying. Many myths insist that merpeople of any type are entirely evil by nature, snatching the bodies and souls of anyone who would peer into the ocean or lake, dragging them down into a watery doom.

Although mermen lore exists, it's easy to see how mer-lore is associated with the perceived "dangers and allure" of women and women's power through the centuries. Mermaids who seduce men with the stare of their glassy eyes mimic the image of the dark enchantress, targeted during the period known as the Inquisition.

What could such a mysterious and maligned being have to teach us about power in the study of Witchcraft? I think that depends on your relationship to the feminine and watery mysteries as they stand now and where you aim to go with them.

One who is disconnected from the feminine lunar ways might be under the impression that merpeople are fearsome watery vampires. On the other hand, someone who is in right relationship with this energy might benefit from the cooperation of the merpeople. Finding hidden things, seeking beauty and "diving deeper" into spiritual pursuits are ideals held sacred by this mystical race of beings.

Neck/Nix

The neck come from the legends and tales of the peoples of Northern Europe and Germany. The neck are often seen as draconian in form and are sometimes compared to the salamander spirits of fire. Like the merpeople, they're known for appearing in human form, shapeshifting being one of their prime abilities.

The name probably comes from nykr, a Scandinavian word meaning "river horse". Looking at the art from people who present them make this a sensible term to use for these mysterious creatures. The Scandinavians weren't very fond of them, claiming that their alluring music would draw pregnant women and unbaptized children to an early, watery grave.

In Germany, the Nix morphed into water-sprites that took on a more ambiguous nature. Jacob Grimm in the nineteenth century wrote of how the water sprites would lure any unsuspecting passerby into the waters, but could also be symbolic of higher beings shapeshifting into animal form.

To me, the neck represented the fears inherent within the shadowy realms of water. Do we dare pass by the river of beauty and risk mortal peril? Meditating upon the nix challenges us to ask ourselves what lies buried deep within the soul. What rests deep within the dark waters may not be what we think.

Gazing the waters - art of scrying

There are few magickal arts so closely connected with water as scrying. Peering into a cauldron filled with water or into a murky lake is a practice steeped within the most mysterious reaches of history.

Hydromancy is the proper term we give for divination by water and is a method much beloved by Witches around the world. The most common form would have a black cauldron filled with water for the scryer to peer into. A chalice or cup could be substituted for a cauldron, or even a simple boiling pot of water on the stove for the modern Witch. With this, the most simple of instruments are transformed into powerful tools for tapping into visions of other worlds.

What exactly happens when we scry? This is often debated but a few things are certain. The diviner's act of gazing into the reflective surfaces causes the mind to go into an alpha-state, that mode you enter when doing "numbing activities" like watching TV or reading a highly engaging book. The alpha-state we're looking for in scrying is quite the opposite of a numbing activity. Rather, we're activating the parts of ourselves that tend to be pushed down by the conscious mind. Ruled by water, the subconscious mind comes alive when we do a little reworking of our sensual surroundings.

What role does water play in this? Water is the most unknown surrounding. Scientists know that like the ocean, humans have only discovered tiny portions of what the mind is capable of. We have some ideas about what it could do if it were fully active, but we really have no clear sense of it. I firmly believe that divination through scrying is one of those untapped sources of mental power that we will all come to know in the days when the human brain is fully engaged. When we think about the high percentage of the human brain that is water (as much as 78 percent), it is clear to see that this powerful element is the key to unlocking the secrets of our full mental potential.

Exercise - Water scrying

First, obtain a vessel for the scrying. It's best if it is some kind of dark bowl with a large circumference (I prefer 10 inches or larger) and a deep bottom. If you have a cauldron, that would be a fantastic tool as it is already infused with the powers of your previous workings. If you prefer a smaller vessel, you might stick with the chalice cup for this.

Next you'll need to consider the scenery of your scrying room. Traditionally, scrying is done in a dark room with a single candle lit behind the scryer or behind the scrying vessel. Personally, I prefer to have the room as dark as possible without even a single candle. At other times, a candle lit far behind me works well too. After scrying for a while you'll come to adopt a particular set of surroundings that work best for you. It's good to experiment, switch things up, and keep the mind guessing.

We can already assume by the title of this section that pure and simple water is usually the fluid put into the scrying vessel. As a modern and artistic Witch, I sometimes like to get creative and switch this up a little. Why not use regular water as a base, but add things to it to enhance the experience. I think anything that will make our work pack an extra punch is worth trying out, don't you?

When we get into custom water types for scrying, the possibilities seem endless. I'll share a few of my favorite things, but I challenge you to experiment with your own formulas and find one that will work better than mine.

Herbal Infusions - An herbal infusion is like a tea. Simply steep the herb of choice in hot water and strain the herb out when done. For scrying, select herbs that have lunar and psychic properties like mugwort, wormwood, and rose. Try to not make the infusion too heavy (this can happen if you use too much herb or let it steep for too long). Having a murky infusion could confuse your visions. Is that a twisted skull foretelling death in your vessel, or is it a stray piece of root you forgot to strain out? You get the picture.

Gem Elixirs - We'll talk in more detail about these in our section on earth, but gem elixirs can be quite useful for scrying fluids where you want to keep the sight of the water clear. To make the elixir, place a charged stone of your choosing in a bowl of water. For scrying, I like to use moonstone or amethyst. For an added bonus, set the bowl out under the light of the full moon to charge over night or on one of the sacred sabbat days. Samhain would be a fantastic time for this.

Holy and Blessed Waters - Don't already bless all the water you work with? This is a great time to start! If you don't normally make your own holy water, using it for scrying will simultaneously bless you as you carry out your work. This has the added side benefit of opening up your higher self to receive visions that are of the most correct and impactful nature. Working with blessed divine energy in scrying invites the forces of nature to bless all our endeavors beyond what we see to be true right in front of us.

To create holy water, obtain a bottle of spring or distilled water and some sea salt. I like Himalayan sea salt. Hold your hands over the water (you can actually do this while the water is directly in the scrying bowl) and come into your center. On every out breath, call upon your light to radiate outwards from your hands, encircling the vessel. The light will slowly begin to swirl about and sink into the water, mingling with it and making it bright. Sometime within this process, add a few pinches of the sea salt and stir with your finger, continuing to add light as you do. I like to use this invocation:

Creature of water, arise and come unto this work
let the pure beauty of your nature flow into this vessel
let all things be made holy by its touch.

Creature of earth, arise and come unto this work
let the pure strength of your being flow into this vessel
let all things be sanctified by its touch.

So mote it be.

Eventually the light will naturally begin to dim and this is when you know the blessing can be done. At this point, you can either put the water away or begin scrying right then. You might even take a moment before scrying to anoint parts of your body (especially the third eye) before you begin your work.

Now it's time to begin the scrying process. Start out by entering a deep meditative state. Go deep, but not deep enough where you can't maintain the vision of your physical surroundings. I recommend breath work that is done with eyes open. You want your eyes to adjust to what you're looking at so that you can intentionally lose focus on it later on. Seven cycles of in and out breaths should do the trick, but don't rush it.

As you continue to fall into a light trance state, allow your eyes to relax while still open. If you've ever looked at the page of a book and willed your eyes to make the words blurry, this is the same type of effect we're going for. This is simply allowing the eyes to go unfocused and there isn't anything especially mystical about that. Controlling what we do with this state is what makes it a powerful act.

As you continue to breath and your eyes lose focus, they will probably snap back into focus on and off at first. This is natural and is just your brain telling your eyes that they need to be in "proper normal vision." This is the conscious part of the brain and can take a back seat for now. Allow your gaze to soften as you stare into the pool of water in your vessel.

This is where it can get tricky, the waiting. You're actually doing several things here, but the ego will probably tell you you're getting bored after a few minutes of nothing happening. It is essential to be patient and give it time. As the conscious parts of you take a rest, your psychic parts will begin to stir. This is where you might start seeing shapes or smoky forms emerge within the depths of the vessel. Again, the eyes will probably try to focus on that. Will your eyes to stay relaxed and let the images do their thing as they swirl around. If you do, the vague shapes should start to take form into solid images. If you're lucky (or practice enough) they may even form entire scenes. This is the ultimate goal and usually comes after several dedicated sessions. You'll notice that the more you see, the more the "visions" are happening in your mind's eye rather than the physical eye. This is really what scrying does for us. It is a tool that unlocks the hidden mysteries of what the brain has the ability to do naturally.

Scrying is a wonderful regular practice that will get you in touch with the spirit of water quickly. After scrying for a while, your dreams will start to improve in clarity, as will your regular waking intuition. These are all gifts of the water realms that we can claim if we choose to receive them.

Dream work

Scrying is almost entirely intentional, but dreaming is mostly not. We can most easily choose to dream on purpose, but it's much harder to choose not to dream. If scrying is like a gentle stream, then dreaming is like opening a flood gate.

That's not to say that dreams can't be channeled of course. In fact, I'd wager that most of us learn about intentional dream magick quite early on in our practice. For many of us though, this ancient and mysterious art can fall to the way-side as we explore other more tangible forms of divination and spiritual communication.

Coming back to intentional dream work (or increasing in practice) can be a highly beneficial thing. Dreaming with memory helps to increase our proficiency with walking between the worlds. It engages the wild and untamed parts of our watery sides that can't often be controlled. Because we have less control over dreaming than we do with scrying, it gives us great experience with working with the waters of the untamed, crossing into many other facets of our lives.

When we dream more, our imaginations become highly

engaged. When the imagination is on high, magick has greater opportunity to flow. Since dreaming has a larger container than scrying, you can hold bigger levels of psychic energy. This can have some drawbacks too. Having a larger container means having to work harder to get it to do what you want.

Divination's connection with emotion

The more adept you become in this art form the more your other intuitive processes will increase along the way. Water rules over divination skills because it also rules over emotion. Psychic power and the power of the heart are both intricately connected. Love and the desire to see what is beyond the physical stem from the mystical powers of the heart charka and flow up into the third eye.

It is well known that children with a highly emotional nature have increased natural psychic ability. This is seen in the many instances of poltergeist activity that actually resulted from a child's early trauma or other experiences that had a strain on their mental and emotional wellbeing. This doesn't stop in childhood though. Many witches who start their craft as teenagers note that their magick seems to work almost instantaneously. Speaking from my own experiences I certainly know this to be the case.

Understanding how psychic energy within the emotions is connected will help us better control all of them. Connecting with the element of water really is the key to an emotionally healthy and psychically healthy existence. When psychic energy and emotional energy are flowing through the heart in a balanced way, the third eye and heart energize the upper part of our bodies, allowing the higher self to communicate in a clearer way.

Emotional energy that is not balanced with psychic energy can have a clear effect on the person's mental and emotional wellbeing. Take for instance the highly eccentric psychic we might see reading on a busy city sidewalk. She may give a hell of a good reading, but she doesn't seem all that "there" either. This is because of the disconnection of power that doesn't have an efficient circuit to run through.

On the flip side, psychic energy that is unbalanced with emotional energy can have an equally damaging effect. Someone who is a newlywed head over heels in love might find that their dreams are always one sided or that they can't give themselves a reading that's up to the level of quality they're used to.

To ensure that our psychic and emotional bodies are acting in a holistic way, you must do work that always engages the entire psychic mind and the emotional heart. We can do this a number of ways of course. Journaling daily about our many emotions and practicing a daily divination are some obvious practices. But what if we worked extra hard to tone these muscles? Imagine what our emotional state would be like. We would no longer be jolted around by every up and down that comes our way.

Exercise - Tuning the psychic and emotional bodies

Begin by focusing on the heart. You might even physically feel it by pressing on it and experiencing the beat that it makes. Feel it pumping the blood all through you. Begin to imagine that pulsing with the bright green energy of the heart chakra. Feel this energy expand until it encompasses your whole lower torso. Imagine what it feels like to experience the full richness of all your emotions at once. Does it feel painful? Does it feel joyful? Let whatever feeling arises within you to simply be.

Next, begin to imagine the third eye. You might even tap it with your forefinger and your index finger. Imagine it glowing bright violet and other purple shades. Feel this energy expand until it encompasses your whole upper torso and head. Imagine what it feels like to have supreme universal psychic power. What would that be like? You would know all that was, all that is, and all that ever will be.

Now begin to make a light humming sound with your voice. As you hum, imagine the energy of the third eye and the heart slowly approaching each other. Visualize the colors as they begin to merge, forming a vesica pisces type of image. Continuing to hum, notice whatever feelings arise in the body or spirit. A slight tingling would be a likely sensation.

Eventually, these powers will merge together fully. When they do, feel free to sit in this place of pure psychic and emotional balance. We can be in this place at all times if we choose to. Our only challenge lies within accessing the still points within the heart and the third eye, and maintaining positive equilibrium throughout our body.

I truly believe that many of the emotional imbalances many people have are a result of psychic imbalances that we simply need to be aware of and correct. One of my teachers talks about how many of our frustrations arise when we try to predict everything in our lives. This is a true consequence of psychic-emotional imbalance.

Illusion

There is illusion all around us, says The Moon tarot card. The waters can mislead and confuse. The beautiful looking mermaid could be the death of you. The waters above might look calm while a powerful under current resides just below the surface.

Water can teach us about looking past illusion, into the vision of what is really there. Its reflective surface challenges us to look at ourselves and the image we present to the world. It tells us that only a person of truth will have the truth shine back to them. What about you seems murky and polluted? What can be done to clear up the waters of our inner channels?

Now is a time to take stock of the current we're standing in. Where does it pull you? How strong or gentle is the force of it? Knowing the nature of the flow we stand in can help us better determine where we're heading. If the waters are clear and flowing at a pace you can swim with, that's how you know you're heading towards your true authentic self.

Sometimes it feels as though the waters around us will never be clear enough to peer into. Sometimes it seems like nothing is true and all around us is an illusion. Communion with water empowers us to see past the facade and down into the bedrock of the ocean floor. What sits there, in its truest form? Will you join it?

Start this work by continuing to keep yourself authentic. Integrity creates a clean channel for a clear stream of consciousness to pass through. Keep people around you who strive to stand in the flow of their great work. Toast to the Old Ones and ancestors often. They will help you sail the sometimes choppy waters. Stand with strength but stretch often and be willing to slowly bend in the directions needed. Trust your gut - water always knows where it's supposed to go.

Physical water - concerns and communion

Like earth and air, our physical water bodies need care or we'll all be in serious trouble. Most people today don't even know the name of their local watershed. As cities grow toxic waste runoff from urban developments causes irreparable damage to rivers, streams, lakes, and oceans.

We all know that water comprises the majority of our physical bodies. We need to consume it every single day to survive. Because of this, it is important that Witches learn how to help with the local water bodies in their area.

You don't have to be an activist or an environmental biologist to do this. Simply becoming aware of the water bodies in your area is the first step to coming into a conversation with those bodies. Communing with water in this way will transmute some of those physical pollutants.

Try it yourself. Visit any sort of local water body near your own home. Find out what its name is. Learn about other bodies of water it connects to. What sort of wildlife make their home in and around that water? When you arrive at the location, sit there and ask it any questions that come to mind. If you have worked with any of the elementals or creatures of water, call upon them now.

Sit there for as long as you need to. It might be a good idea to bring some kind of environmentally friendly gift there. Record your experiences and visit this water often.

The bodily benefits of communing with water in this way are many. You might notice that water tastes better or that you need less of it before you feel thirsty. Libation and the ritual consumption of water will increase this.

The art of ritual libation

The most intimate connection that many of us have in ritual with water is at the time of the ritual libation. Libation is an act of pouring and consuming a toast in honor of the gods and the sacred divine within each of us. In covens, this usually consists of passing around the chalice filled with wine and saying "thou art goddess, may you never thirst". A sip of the wine is then taken and passed on to the next person. In solitary ritual this usually just consists of drinking the contents of the chalice and pouring the rest on the ground.

Ritual libation is quite the ancient practice. Ritual goblets have been discovered all over the world aged thousands of years old. The act of libation is a sacrifice to the gods and a symbol of our connection to them here on earth. Libation tells the gods that we have something to give back.

The libation can be formed with any type of fluid (usually wine), simple water is the most basic and probably the most natural form. When drinking from all-water goblets in ritual, you can then pour the resulting water on the ground or in a bowl before you. If it's not the kind of water you ingest (such as holy water), you can keep a stock of the water near at your altar space and give a libation at any time. You might even have a separate reserve of water set aside specifically for this.

We know what libation symbolizes to the gods, but what does it do for our practice in particular? For one, it gives us an intimacy with water that's different to the intimacy we experience when we drink it. When we consume water we are always taking it in. Libation is a conscious return. In giving water back to the land we are acknowledging the sacred cycle of give and take, ebb and flow, send and receive. Think about it this way; when you make a toast to a friend, it's usually for some special joyous occasion. A libation is nothing more than a toast put into the spiritual context that honors the divine. It tells the gods that something special has just happened or will happen. It tells our minds that our conversation with the divine is being strengthened by this act.

I know many Witches who only practice libation at their coven meetings or other major festivals. Personally I think this is rather a waste. Why not toast to the gods all the time? Regular libation is not only enacted as worship to your gods, but it's also a form of the active engagement with the water elementals.

The chalice - which is the most common vessel for libation - is the classical weapon of water. It holds our wishes, our prayers, and our gratitude. Even Christianity recognizes the power of the chalice. In Christian lore, one of the most sacred objects is the cup Christ drank from at the last supper. Legend says it was dropped into the waters of the chalice well gardens in Glastonbury, England. Due to the content of the well's iron ore, the water shimmers with somewhat of a red tint. Pagans say this is really the blood of the earth mother flowing through the veins of the land at this most sacred site.

The drinking goblet can be a weapon of harm too. A very common method of poisoning centuries ago was by way of poison in the cup of a dinner guest. Like any weapon, the chalice only exerts its power in the way we direct it to.

Exercise - Performing a communal libation

This exercise can be done during ritual or as a ritual on its own. All you need is some type of drinking vessel. Really, that's it.

I prefer to do this out doors where I can directly pour the libation onto the earth when I'm done. If this is impossible, you can pour the water into a bowl on your altar for removal later on. Try to make sure that the liquid you're using is used only for this purpose. The sanctity of your vessel's liquid is the most important physical consideration.

Begin by touching the water with the tips of your fingers as you come into a place of stilled communion. In your process, you might make the water holy as we discussed earlier.

When ready, hold the chalice high and say aloud:

Oh blessed creature of water, be here with me in this rite.
charge this offering and make it holy.
Beloved of the ancestors and in the hall of the gods, I make this
sacred libation.
The moon knows of the gifts of water. I bring them down and offer
them up.
Bless this gesture oh Holy Ones, and may it be pleasing to you.

You can then pour the water into another vessel or right onto the ground. In a libation of gratitude, this would be the time when you would reflect on the blessings you received.

Riding the wave

We have covered communing with water in the mental, physical and psychic methods. Connection with water is truly an interesting process. Some may think fire takes the most courage to work with, but I think water wins the award when it comes to the bravery required to do this work. When we're high on water, we can feel like we're riding on a wave of pure joy that nothing can stop. When we're at a low point, we feel all the hardships of our emotional body and everything that comes with that. Working with water won't always be easy, but it's a powerful and important step towards elemental mastery.

Elemental mastery with water can put a stressed out heart at ease. The gifts of water are many. Union with water means reclaiming the power to love and be loved in return. When we have this power, truly nothing can stand in our way. We become invincible forces of compassion, guiding the waters of our lives with flexibility and adaptation.

As we approach our last element, we will use the lessons of water to complete the elemental circle by blending the four together. As we have the right of the waves of elemental connection, we will become a part of all around us.

Chapter 4

Earth

The soil is the great connector of our lives, the source and destination of all.
- Wendell Berry

Earth is what I consider to be the most complex and intriguing element. When we think of earth we can think of two things; our planet called Earth, and the actual stuff Earth has as its base, soil and rock. In this way, saying "earth" can really mean the culmination of all four physical elements. For the purpose of this discussion we'll refer to earth as the physical ground beneath our feet and the mountainous forms that rise up above us.

If there was an element most associated with the religion of the Witch, it would be earth. After all, we're usually called an "earth-based" faith. The Witch knows that earth connection is essential to having a grounded anchor for our magick to manifest. When earth supports our work, we have a foundation for lift-off.

Earth to the Witch is a home base. When we start and end magickal workings, we always come back to earth. When we perform astral travel or heal at a distance, earth is where we draw our energy and send it out. Knowing that all people are on the earth in some way (unless you're flying in an airplane or skydiving) helps us establish an energetic link when we do magick with the desire to affect someone else. Earth is the great leveler. From it we emerge and unto it we will all return.

When we look at the historical origins of the Witch in Europe, we see that he is usually associated with earthen practices in some way. She is the village healer, using knowledge of herbs and stones to tend to the sick. He is often seen living in deep wooded forests or at the edge of a mountain range. The oracles at the Temple of Apollo at Delphi resided close to a cave where they would summon up mysterious visions from mist forming at the fissure crack in the rock. Inscribed within the temple's forecourt was the now famous aphorism "know thyself". If I had to think of one simple phrase to describe the element of earth, that would be it. The reason why the Witch is considered a "wise one" is because we are always being challenged to know ourselves and all around us with increasing depth and understanding throughout our lives. With this self-knowledge comes the power to have knowledge and conversation with all things. When we connect with all things, anything is possible.

In earth we see the great cycles of nature and the effects it has on all other elements. Though the cycle of the seasons rely on the sun, our seasons would become stagnant if it weren't for the movement of the earth. For that reason I like to associate the mysteries of death and rebirth with the turning of the earth. It is from these mysteries that some of our most powerful ideas arise. What animates the unfurling of the leaves in spring time? How does the soil create the environment needed for seeds to germinate before sprouting? What within us must exist within the below before it can poke its head into the surface?

The Eleusinian Mysteries teach this and much more. These ideas originating from ancient Greece center on the cult of Demeter and Persephone and their stories of Earth changes. These mysteries refer to the myths surrounding the goddess Demeter and her famous descent into the Underworld.

The myth of the descent of Persephone
- the short version

Persephone (also known as Kore, or Maiden) is the young and beautiful daughter of the mighty earth goddess Demeter. Demeter, having the busy duty of taking care of the growth of all things on the earth, was highly protective of her daughter who she couldn't always keep a close eye on.

One day while picking wildflowers grown by her mother, the fearsome king of the Underworld appeared before her. Some say she was entranced by his presence and went willingly with him. Others say she was violently seized and taken captive. Some even believe that Persephone's decision had very little to do with Hades at all and was simply her desire to explore new lands and experience a new life. I am attracted to that version. Whichever version you follow, Persephone leaves the world of surface and sunshine and makes her journey into the dark place, the Underworld.

In the throes of anger and grief, Demeter mourned and caused a terrible drought upon the earth and thus the first winter began. This caused the mortal people to languish and suffer. Zeus, seeing that the suffering humans were losing faith, pleaded with Demeter to end the cold spell. Zeus agreed to overrule Hades' legal ties and negotiated for Persephone to return to the surface to visit her mother for six months out of the year. When Persephone is with her mother, the earth springs back into life as Demeter celebrates. When it is time for Persephone to return to the depths, Demeter once again mourns and the earth is thrown into darkness.

When we look at this story through the lens of earth magick, we see that earth is both fearful and fruitful. It is seen by Demeter as a prison for her daughter, yet also a cause for triumph when she is freed. This to me very much represents the views of being grounded in both eastern and western culture. Many teachings of the east state that the ultimate goal is total detachment from the earth, heading towards a place of pure ascension. In the west, it seems that the goal is often the opposite, striving for mastery of the physical word, achieving spiritual union through that bonding process with the physical. The Witch in any culture believes that neither view is wholly true or wholly false.

We can become both rooted in the physical, while stretching up towards the sky. The cosmos is alive in both spaces and the gods speak through both simultaneously. Elemental connection through earth teaches us how to be in that place of co-existence. Through the tools of earth work, we find our still point, ground towards our core, and pull up the nourishment needed to do our Great Work.

Exercise - Descending into the cave

We can experience a form of Persephone's descent by working with the power of cave imagery in journey work. Caves are known to be portals to the Otherworld and are thresholds into the mysterious world of earth power.

To journey deep within the earth, you'll need to achieve a deep state of relaxed meditation, almost to the point of sleep, but not quite. You might even want to lie down on your back if you're confident that you won't actually fall asleep. For your background, it's helpful to have very dim lighting (or no light at all) with some slow and steady drumming playing softly in the background. To enhance the experience, try burning earthy incense such as sandalwood or patchouli.

As you enter your deepest meditative state, imagine the opening of a cave before you. I like to imagine it centered deep within a dark and lush forest. This cave will be no ordinary cave. It might be adorned with special sigils or runes indicating a doorway to the deep Otherworld. Notice your surroundings before you enter so you can establish an anchor for your way out.

Slowly approach the cave entrance, continuing to slow your breathing and the fluttering of thoughts that might be passing through the mind. I find it helpful to linger at the cave entrance for a time if I feel that my thoughts need a few moments to pass by.

When you're ready, pass through the mouth of the cave and surrender to the cool darkness that surrounds you. It smells damp and rocky and the only sounds are of the wind whistling past and a couple of drops of water from the roof. Take in the sensory experiences and move forward.

As you walk forward, feel yourself going down. It might be a downward steady slope or something carved out like a spiral staircase. Let your imagination take over as you walk further down into the depths of the earth. Take note of anything you find along the way. You might find a special stone or a plant growing in your path. Those are likely to be gifts from the spirits of the earth, greeting you as you enter their domain. If you feel called to, pick them up and place them in your pocket or bag for safe keeping.

When you feel like you can go no further, you might find yourself in a circular space, dimly lit but with all the features and symbols of the earthen surface adorning the walls. This is the temple of the earth element, where the power of the earth elementals arise and return. Take a moment in this space to say a prayer or explore the sights.

If you're lucky, perhaps an earth spirit will greet you while in this space. If one does, be still and pay attention in case it has a message for you. If there is no message, you can simply take a bow in honor before you leave.

When you're ready to return, trace your steps back up the slope or staircase towards the surface. Be as slow and deliberate going up as you were when going down. Again, take notice of any sights alone the way. When you reach the surface, you cross through the cave mouth and are once again aglow in the gentle light of the lush forest or other scene that you came up with.

As you leave the area, check and see if you brought anything back with you. Did you have a gift from the temple of earth? If so, open it up in your hand and take a look. Know that when you awaken, you will have this gift for safe keeping in your astral toolbox.

Since cave journeying is incredibly grounding, you might feel the need to drink some water or get some fresh air afterwards. I like to eat something sweet to snap me back into balance, like a piece of fresh fruit. Journeying for earth power at regular intervals will help you get more acquainted with the elementals (who we'll discuss shortly) and the power they gift the world with every day.

Finding and sitting in stillness

The reason why so many struggle with meditation can often be traced to issues of stillness. Our culture likes to tell us that it's not good to be still. We have to be constantly moving and constantly "doing." This busy culture fails to recognize that due to the electrical buzz of all molecules, all things are moving at all times whether we direct them to or not. When we slow down enough to have a physical stillness, we give room for that buzz inside and around us to expand. This buzzing (I have heard it called "The God Frequency"), is the vehicle for energetic expansion. When we work magick, we are changing the frequency of this buzz so that it vibrates in the octave we need it do.

Mountains speak well of stillness. Though they are constantly changing and re-shaping, we usually cannot see it with our limited human sight. As plates shift and the landscape changes, the mountain stands where it is while allowing change to occur in more subtle ways. This is how it survives. If it were to shift and move its entire form every time a movement ruptured through it, it would be difficult for anything on its surface to find a stable home. The trees would have trouble taking root and animals wouldn't consider it safe enough to dwell in. Because the mountain has stillness, we find value in its ability to simply *be*.

We can become like the mountain. There's even a pose in yoga just for it. We can tell the world that we have the right to be still when we need to be. This takes discipline, commitment and insistence. We have to really brain ourselves to be ok with sitting in stillness. Once we give permission, the body and soul will take us there. In this busy world and within our busy lives, they really crave to be there. This is why some people experience intense euphoric feelings of joy and bursts of energy when they finally learn how to sit still and meditate properly. That rush of energy comes when we pause long enough for that divine spark within us to grow a little brighter and get a little hotter.

To first find physical stillness, a couple of things are required. First, it is helpful to practice good posture. If you ignored everything your mother told you, at least remember the part about sitting up straight. If you're not used to having good posture, it won't feel very comfortable at all at first. Give it time. After a week or so of consciously remembering to keep the spine upright and elongated, it will start to feel a little more natural. In addition to helping our bodies find stillness, this good posture will also be extremely helpful at helping the breath flow to all the right places. This leads us to the second requirement, breath.

As we discussed in the air chapter, breath is pretty essential to all effective magickal acts, no matter what we're doing. Just as breath can activate and stir great power within, so too can it drop power down and keep us grounded. In finding stillness, deep slow breaths are the best. I like to do a count of seven. The count of seven would be in whatever second that makes the most sense for the comfort level of your lungs. So the pattern would go; in for seven, hold for seven, out for seven, hold again for seven, repeat. You can do this series a couple of times quickly. I like to do it seven times or longer when I desire a very deep sense of stillness.

After finding good posture and the flow of a slow breath, you are probably already in a still place or very close to it (at least physically).

The next part is on the mental and etheric levels. Even though the body feels still, we can still have a lot going on in our brains. The "mental chatter" that so many people struggle with in meditation is probably the hardest part of finding stillness and finding it quickly. To help with this, I like to do a simple visual when the chatter is too much to just forget about. Earth power will help us with this and we can focus on it to lead us there.

Going back to our mountain reference, you can actually visualize part of you as a mountain, with the base sloping down to the bottom of your behind. You might even take it a step further to imagine your bones as bedrock and your skin as the feel of the grass. The hairs on your head could be as branches of the trees. The other option is to imagine one of the many symbols that correspond with the earth as an element.

You can choose to focus on the symbol for the entire length of time, or you can start out focusing on it and then let it fade into the background of your mind until you have a "blank slate" image.

Continuing to practice stillness will result in achieving the state quicker and with more ease. When I practice this regularly and really commit to it, I can drop into stillness in a matter of seconds. Being able to find stillness in seconds is a fabulous tool to have. For people with high stress careers, being able to drop into stillness immediately can increase productivity, reduce blood pressure (and stress as a result), and improve the quality of whatever you're doing. No matter what you do, starting out from stillness means you will proceed with a solid anchor throughout your entire process.

What happens when we come out of stillness and lose our anchor? Drop into it again. The outside stressors don't want you to be still. The negative energy trying to feed off you counts on you not having a strong anchor. If you lose your place and need to stop and go back to find it again, do it. There isn't any rule that says you can't find a still place on a repeated number of times for as long as you need. Only you can dictate when you need to go there. And the more you do it, the more you'll take notice of times when you need to do it.

Grounding your body, grounding your work

Grounding takes your practice one step further. Grounding is what happens when we not only touch upon stillness and draw strength from it, but when we totally become rooted in that space long enough to become merged with it for a time.

For many people who perform ritual, grounding is always a necessary step. We know that it is essential for the effective flow and direction of our energy both before and after any ritual process. Yet still, it amazes me how rushed some of these grounding exercises for ritual can be. The other issue is that ritual leaders sometimes don't take a moment to see if everyone has reached a grounded place before moving on. This can result in a ritual that is unfocused and scattered, or even exhaustive for the entire group.

Focusing on grounding as a deeply important step will help us ensure that everyone is starting out at the same solid anchor point. Those who take a little longer to ground are often also people who have an uncanny ability to raise an extraordinary amount of energy in ritual. Using the full potential of these people is a great asset to working magick or inducing ritual consciousness. The ungrounded energy raiser is a waste to the working and it's really a shame to experience a ritual where their full abilities are not recognized and put into place.

Effective grounding means that we are literally merging with the ground beneath our feet. Even if we're on a rooftop, we can still "pull up" the earth to meet us. Just because the earth is solid doesn't mean its essence isn't mutable. When we ground long enough to merge with the earth, we take a little bit of it with us when we engage in our practice, whatever that may be. Taking a piece of that earth with you means you'll have the strength and intelligence of that power to guide your away. And as we discussed before, anything we can do to have more power in our work is always going to be something we want to pay attention to.

Grounding, beyond tree and roots

Most magickal practitioners know of the common "tree and roots" exercise for grounding. The practitioner imagines roots growing down from either the base of the spine or the feet, with branches extending upwards from raised arms or the top of the head. The person then takes in energy from above, passes it through their being, and then lets it sink into the earth below through the roots. There are a few variations to this but that's the basic form of it.

While tree and roots is a great tool to have, there are some pretty interesting ways to expand upon it and take it to the next level. The tricky part about tree and roots is that there isn't a full merging process with it. You only have these small extensions of yourself rising up and falling below. When you're done getting what you need, the astral appendages sink back into the physical body. What would happen if we put all of us into the earth? That's the kind of grounding that forges a lasting anchor.

While doing basic grounding, we often forget that earth is mutable just like all the other elements. We forget that the planet is constantly moving just as much as the soil beneath. The idea of earth being totally fixed - though helpful - is an illusion. Because of this, we can call upon earth to rise up and meet us half way.

The earth will do this because it supports our work. It supports our work because it too benefits from our having an authentic grounding experience. When we "ground down", we're fertilizing the energetic body of the earth with something it doesn't get enough of - healing. With this in mind, we ground knowing that the element of earth responds well to reciprocity. When we give, it gives back. This is true in both the physical and etheric sense. We give it water, it gives us food crops. You get the picture.

The next time you start with tree and roots, experiment with it. Instead of putting "roots" all the way down, will the ground beneath you to literally rise up around you as you sink beneath the surface. This is a wonderfully intriguing exercise to do while lying on your back, especially directly on the ground outside.

Imagine yourself becoming like a liquid gel slipping through the pores of the soil down into the earth's crust and mantle. Fully imagine every layer of the earth as you rest and breathe within each one. What does each layer feel like? Is it hot or cold? Wet or dry? Firm or soft? Is there a layer you feel like you can't get past once you get there? Some people might like to go to the very core of the earth. For grounding, I would advise against this as the core has such fierce fire energy you might defeat the purpose of the exercise as you risk bringing that back with you.

When ready, you simply will your porous body to lift back up like a helium balloon until you get back to the surface. This is so incredibly grounding that you might not even want to get up! If that happens, simple breathe in some energy right from the sky above you until you feel leveled out.

Checking in

Checking in is when you take a brief moment to re-center, re-ground, and re-sync yourself up with all your parts. It's like performing a mini tune up on the body, mind, and spirit at various points in the day. Consider it like taking a coffee break, but drinking the type of coffee that will give you more than just a physical buzz.

Checking in is helpful primarily because we all lead busy lives. The modern Witch might not be able to live the type of lifestyle that allows him to pray and work magick all throughout the day. We have jobs, families and a myriad of other commitments that need tending to. Simply finding one time in the day for full sitting practice can be enough of a challenge on its own without finding time in the middle of the day to do it again.

This is where this tune up is helpful. You can condense nearly any of the practices we've discussed so far into a one minute working. Keep in mind that this will be much more effective if you have done the full version of that working prior in the day, but every little bit helps. Condensing an exercise when you need to doesn't decrease the value of it. Rather, it places more value on the act because you're valuing the need for it within the rush of your busy day. Sacrificing that one or two minutes within your busiest time of day means you're declaring your right to be a sovereign, self-possessed being.

Checking in falls under the domain of earth because earth teaches us about effective time management as spiritual creatures. People usually think of time management today as techniques to squeeze as much "stuff" into a time window as possible. Companies that put on expensive time management trainings to do this really miss the mark. Truly effective time management is looking at the time you have and realistically assessing what you can do with it. Everyone gets the same amount of minutes in the day. Grounding, centering, and energizing should all be part of those minutes.

What does a typical check in look like? That is really up to you. Like your daily sitting practice, you should tailor your own check in sessions to reflect what you need them to be. And like regular sitting practice, it will likely change over time. I do a number of things when I check in, yet it changes more frequently than my sitting practice does. Remember that since this is just a little tune up in your day, you don't have to have as strict a regimen as you might normally set for yourself.

I also like to style the check in based on what my day is going like. If my work day is absolute insanity, I focus on deep grounding. I might do heavy in-breaths, taking in all the fiery energy around my office and channeling it down into the earth. If I feel unfocused and unable to concentrate for whatever reason (usually around 2:00 p.m. on a Friday for me), I might drop into my center by sensing that still point in my core and breathing into the awareness of it for a moment.

I do these things at my desk, in the kitchen, or even in the bathroom stall depending on what I'm planning to do. Whenever I remember to check in, I find that my stress is reduced and my productivity increases. During weeks when I have a heavy schedule, I specifically schedule a few minutes a few times a day to check in. I will literally set an electronic reminder on my computer calendar that says "stop, drop, and check in!" I might also pair the reminder with a list of short exercise suggestions. My list looks something like this:

Breathe for three counts of three Ground by quickly "pulling up" the earth around/beneath me Holding a dense stone to my forehead like hematite or obsidian. Roll energizing stones around in the palm of the hand such as amber and jet. Sense out the chakras, sending a quick in-breath to each one. Visualize flaming blue pentacles around me, burning away negativity if there is any around me at the time. Tilt the head up, breathe in, tilt the head down, breath out. This aligns with earth and sky. Say a mantra or short prayer such as "I AM, fully human and fully spirit. I am here. I am now." Charge up a glass of water, making it holy. Drink all or most of it down at once.

After getting into the habit of checking in you'll likely discover new suggestions for yourself. Getting creative and coming up with new ideas will help get you looking forward to your daily check in's.

Earth in alchemy - fermentation

In taking a quick look at the alchemical process, we can arguably associate the process of fermentation with the earth element. You're probably familiar with fermentation in the wine making process where grapes become fermented. In this process, yeast works with the sugars of the juice to create the chemical ethanol and carbon dioxide. In biochemistry, fermentation refers to the extraction of energy from organic material becoming oxidized.

So to put it plainly, fermentation is the decomposition of various parts that result in the release or extraction of energy.

This is an earthen process primarily because of what happens to the body when we die. After we die, the flesh begins to decompose along with the rest of our physical body. In green burials, the organic compounds of the body release nutritional energy into the earth, feeding the soil that surrounds it.

This image reminds us about earth's unsung power of release. Earth has a reputation for the ability to hang onto things. That is partly true, as that's the reason we use earth as a grounding anchor. Yet still, earth also has a fabulous release ability through this process of fermentation.

If you've ever read anything about the Pennsylvania-Dutch pow-wow practices, you might be familiar with their techniques to combat illness with breath and earth. In their process, the pow-wow will make a series of hand passes over the client's body to assess where the illness energy resides. Once they discover the location, they essentially suck in the illness with the breath and then push it onto a spot on the floor. This is the pow-wow opening up a type of energetic vortex for the illness to pass in to. Once it gets sent into this black hole type of space, it gets sent deep into the soil where the earth breaks it up and transmutes it into something useful. This is energetic fermentation and a highly effective method of banishing disease. The specific pow-wow method isn't normally recommended for beginner healers as the healer runs the risk of taking on part of the illness themselves. But done properly, I'd wager that the illness would have a hard time standing up for itself.

In spiritual alchemy, fermentation is usually not considered to be a pleasant process. It can often involve a complete breakdown of the personality as a requirement for the pure gold of the soul to flow through. In spiritual practice, fermentation can be described as the underlying process of the experience called "dark night of the soul." Dark night of the soul is a term used to describe a period of spiritual crisis on the way towards a euphoric breakthrough in spiritual revelation.

Fermentation occurs when we're highly dedicated in prayer work and grounding. It is what happens when we are totally at one with the earth element and give it permission to do with us what it will. It brings up a few questions for us to think about in doing our work with earth. What parts of us need to be broken down to make room for better things? What kind of energy flow would result in that breaking down? Asking yourself these questions would be a good journal prompt in doing your earth work.

Creatures of earth

Gnomes

The gnome is the classic earth elemental that we're all pretty familiar with. It's hard to stroll through a suburban neighborhood without spotting at least one positioned strategically among a garden or grove of trees. Although we consider the gnome a cute American garden decoration, they have quite a colorful history in the lore of the spirit world.

Coming from the Latin and Greek words meaning "earth dweller", they are said to make their homes in trees among dense forest land. Lore states that they have the strength of ten humans and can run at remarkably high speeds to do their duties. Though small, they are said to be one of the strongest elemental creatures when it comes to manipulating physical form.

Gnomes are guardians of green land and protectors of the animals who reside within. Some say they have quite an aversion to all humans in general, while some insist that they're highly friendly to humans being the only elemental creature that takes on a consistently humanoid form.

The gnome carries powerful spiritual medicine. Working with gnomes in magick means practicing commitment and calling upon the full potential of your strength, especially in physical and worldly matters. Because gnomes would usually rather be left alone to do their work, getting in touch with them requires patience and stability, all gifts of the earth. Making a plea to the gnome kingdom for these energies may not be entirely successful the first try, but stick to it. When they notice your persistence and dedication, they're more likely to reach out a helping hand.

Dryads

Dryads are tree spirits and come from Greek mythology. Originally the term dryad was meant to indicate the spirit dwelling within the oak tree specifically. Now the term is often used to describe the spirit of any living tree. They're considered to be a type of nymph in species and some would even call them sprites.

Though not the actual tree itself, the dryad is a being within the tree and both are intrinsically linked. It is said that if a dryad is killed outside of her home tree, that tree will die. The reverse is also true. This makes the dryad a naturally fierce protector of trees and any threat to the livelihood of the wooded area is not likely to be met with any kindness.

Dryads are known for their love of babies and children and are highly interested in their protection. It is for this reason that humans who share the same concern for children are considered to have an easier time approaching a dryad in nature.

In the Celtic version of the dryad, the being is approached before the act of cutting a wand from a tree. Lore states that the dryad is to be asked to temporarily leave the tree (in exchange for a pleasant offering) while the cutting takes place. As a gesture of thanks, the dryad will instill within the wand the power of the tree that it resides over.

Working with dryads is essential when doing magick involving physical trees or within wooded placed. Even if you don't summon them specifically, they should at least be taken into consideration before you begin your work. Having their cooperation means you have the cooperation of the spirit of the forest and your magickal impact will increase exponentially because of it.

The dryad teaches us about our natural connection to the physical world and our responsibility to care for it. We are not separate from the earth and what we do to it, we also do to ourselves. Call upon the dryad with an organic offering at the base of a tree. Ask the dryad to help remind you of your connection to the great Gaian root system we are all a part of. The dryad will likely be delighted by your interest and oblige.

Waldgeist and Kodama

In looking at a less well known earth spirit we come to the waldgeist. Waldgeist translates to "woodland spirit" in Germany and they are believed to be the protectors of these places. Living in tree branches with heads of twigs and leaves, seeing one is considered to be an extremely good omen. They're quite pixie-like in nature and are known for causing harmless mischief to travelers passing through their lands.

In Japan, a very similar spirit exists called the kodama. Like the waldgeist, the kodama protect the forest and are considered quite friendly. However, cutting down a tree where kodama happens to be is thought to be highly ominous and signals dire misfortune to the cutter and his company.

Waldgeist and kodama teach us about the joy of the forest and remind us that the wooded places can be a source of pure delight and rest. They remind us why it's so refreshing to take a walk through a deeply wooded place. The forest is a place of deep power and the joy obtained in visiting one can immediately activate the child-self and that sense of innocent wonder we had as kids.

No matter if you're in a forest or not, you can call upon the waldgeist for general blessings and to protect against misfortune. Images of the waldgeist are carved all over doorways in Germany for this very reason. You can also summon them for activating child-self which is a highly effective grounding technique in itself.

In general, the spirits of earth teach us all about coming into full self-possession by way of the physical form. The body doesn't have to be a limitation to spiritual growth. Rather, it is an important self (among many) needed to be the vehicle for our work and our magick. Living well within the body means we respect each of our selves enough to show up and do the work needed to take care of it.

Earth-walking

Earth-walking is the practice of moving in a way that is mindful of the ground beneath your feet and the energy of the earth formations around you. With literally every step you take, there is a chance for connection with earth. Even city ground covered in layers of concrete is constantly vibrating with this elemental energy, if only we take a moment to look down and see it. Every time we pass by a tree (even the ones cities plant on sidewalks for decoration), we have an opportunity to form a new alliance and gain an energetic ally with the power that inhabits our surroundings.

Native American oral tradition speaks frequently of earth-walking as an essential skill for any hunter. The cunning forest person can walk through a wooded place without making a single sound, because she is fully part of all that surrounds her. When we walk in unison with earth, we actually need to take less specific time out of our day for grounding. When we walk firmly, the grounding becomes part of our natural process simply by walking.

This is primarily done by just paying attention. What does the ground feel like as you walk? Are your shoes thin enough so you can feel the contour of the land or pavement? What is the rhythm of your steps like as each foot hits the ground with a beat? We make music with earth when we walk but we need to tune our eyes and ears properly before we can hear it.

Once you take notice of your physical movement, you can then sense out the psychic energy that comes along with it. Because everything vibrates with energy (especially pure elements), each time you take a step you mingle with that vibration for a second. When you take notice of this, you can take advantage of the energy you touch and ask it to linger within you as you move.

For a visual, you can imagine the soft buzzing energy of earth like a blanket over the ground. With each step you take, feel the dense particles of the ground energy forming an instantaneous bond with your feet, then releasing as the other foot hits the ground. This does a couple of things. First, it somewhat forces you to walk with purpose and mindfulness. Second, it causes hundreds of tiny acts of grounding to occur. It's like doing a tree and roots exercise per every single step you take.

The same type of thing happens when you walk past those trees. You might imagine each branch slowly bending towards you like they're trying to touch you as you walk past. As you breathe, take in the scent of the trees and the lush oxygen it's providing you through its leaves. If it's autumn, you might close your eyes a bit as you walk, taking notice of the sound of the leaves crunching beneath your shoes.

Earth-walking will help us become infused with energy and power simply by walking down the street. The small act of walking down your driveway to take the trash out then becomes a powerful act of magick and meditation. The wise Witch takes in strength at every possible moment.

The mineral kingdom

The Mineral Kingdom refers to stones and minerals and the associations and vibrations they carry. Most of us are introduced to stone work when we first begin to learn about spellcraft. Some stick with those studies and some leave them behind. When I started I had absolutely no interest in working with stones for at least a decade. They just didn't seem to interest me or call to me. I now think it's possible that their vibration just didn't resonate with me for that time.

The vibrations of stones are of the lowest sort in the natural world. Plants operate to a similar degree, but stone energy tends to be almost entirely fixed into place. For a person who is used to working with high vibrational energy, using stones in magickal and spiritual work can be either challenging or just completely uninteresting. I tend to agree with this theory as my personal practice is definitely a reflection of that process.

When Witches work with stones, we are working with several different layers of spiritual bodies. First, we work with the spirit of that type of stone, described by its name. Is this usually what we think of when dealing with the Mineral Kingdom? Additionally though, we're also working with the spirit of that specific stone on its own. There are many ideas about this, but you can think of it like the personality. For people, we have a spiritual body that is always connected in some way to the reflection of the Divine Mind while we still have our own unique personalities that exist within our bodies. The same is true for stones and we might call it their "personal body" spirit. Lastly, each stone has the energy of the place it came from. This can be divided by way of their specific location in their region or as wide as the continent on which it resides. So when we work with a stone, we're also working with the spirit of place where that stone came from.

Witches work with any and every stone they come across. From rocks in the backyard to elaborate gems costing thousands of dollars, some practitioners will spare no expense to get the perfect stone for their vast collection. Though collecting stones can be a fun hobby, I think it's more effective for our practice to work slowly with stones on a one by one basis, developing relationships with them over time. This is important when we think of stones as more than just an inanimate psychic battery for our work. When we regard them as important and powerful spiritual beings in the grand scheme of things, we realize their full potential and can access their full power. Many people have a favorite type of mineral that they tend to collect a lot of. This shows that the personal relationships grown with stones are highly valuable and shouldn't be understated.

Though you can work with any stone you like, there are particular types of minerals that I feel serve the work of the Witch quite well. These stones can hone our craft and make us more effective at raising, directing and grounding energy. If you're just looking into stones deeply, I would recommend any of the stones in the list below to start out with.

Stones and minerals of witchcraft

Agate - Keeps words and thoughts in good order. Many believe agate will cause people to favor you but I think this is more related to its effect on making you a truthful and genuine person. People finding you likeable is just a good side effect from that. I find moss agate particularly helpful as it opens the crown chakra, increasing one's ability to communicate clearly with spirit allies and beings of the Otherworld. This would be a great stone to carry while performing the cave journey exercise.

Amber - Though not actually a stone (it is fossilized tree resin), amber is one of my favorite mineral-like materials to work with. It's thought to be one of the oldest materials to use for jewelry and is much beloved in Traditional Wicca. Amber will generate an electrical charge when rubbed against certain types of cloth and many associate it with pure power for this reason. Sacred to all goddesses, amber is traditionally worn next to jet in alternating sequence as a beaded necklace. Not being one to favor gender norms, I love wearing amber and jet during ritual and find it highly effective at giving an extra energetic boost to my workings.

Amethyst - Probably one of the most popular stones used today. No one can deny the attractiveness of its light to dark purple hues. Although a type of quartz, amethyst usually rests within its own category based in its long reputation within the magickal arts. Most highly regarded as a stone of psychic energy, amethyst can be worn on the upper parts of the body to lift the spirit into a place of conversation with the higher self.

I find this to be a helpful stone to know when I'm doing "emergency magick", or magick that I'm performing under upsetting or urgent circumstances. It acts as a compassionate anchor and ensures that my work is coming from a place of peace and deep understanding. Amethyst can help you relate better to other people and halt interpersonal problems before they occur. A gem elixir featuring amethyst is a fabulous thing to drink before doing many readings or spiritual consultation sessions.

Amazonite - Amazonite holds the nickname of "hope stone" and once you learn more about it, it's easy to see why. There isn't a huge amount of lore concerning amazonite as it's considered to be a "new age" stone and has only recently become easily available. I list this stone here because it encourages faith in both the divine and also the self. Amazonite appropriates self-love like rose quartz, but on a more intimate and multidimensional platform. Amazonite improves faith as it helps you discover the tap into the personal powers that already exist within you.

Aventurine - Aventurine is a stone of opportunity and is set to place us exactly where we need to be for good things to transpire. Energetically, aventurine causes this to happen because it causes the mind to have increased perception. Having increased perception results in knowing which unfolding path to take to result in an immediate blessing. Aventurine is helpful to a Witch of spiritual depth because it can help us make those subtle decisions that change the way we experience each moment in our lives. The unfurling beauty of each day is taking place all around us, if only we have the vision to see it. Aventurine's ability to help us envision a beautiful world helps to inspire our Craft and reach for greatness.

Azurite - Azurite is a vision stone and works by helping the mind release the busy activity and noise that prevents us from being fully present. This is a fantastic stone to use for meditation and general sitting practice as it helps to open you up to new experiences and inspires the mind to do the Great Work. Azurite helps to open the flow of the energy systems in the body and ensures that the various subtle bodies are working together efficiently. Keep azurite on your altar as a focus if you struggle with maintaining a daily sitting practice.

Bloodstone - Bloodstone has a variety of flashy abilities including the power to stop blood from coming out of the body, increasing blood flow within the body, see the truth, win legal battles, inspire bravery, and cure snakebites.

Of particular interest to the Witch is the stone's connection with all the sacred mysteries of the blood. Even Christian lore associates great power to the bloodstone claiming that it was formed from the drops of blood that fell from Christ while on the cross. This gave it the nickname of "martyr's stone." Bloodstone in modern Witchcraft is great to use for summoning up the power of the Witch-blood, our sacred birthright. When Witch-blood is activated, the power of the ancestors and the Might Dead of Witches before us spring into action. Bloodstone reminds us of our eternal connection to all people on the planet and the potential for all people to touch magick.

Citrine - This is a great stone for working with the Will and helps any process revolving around adaptation or change of process. It's particularly useful for helping to release old patterns and the unhelpful "stories" we tell ourselves that stand in the way of our greatness. Highly solar in nature, citrine promotes clarity and puts us in touch with celestial fire and the powers of the sun. As a Leo, I find that this stone enhances the positive associations with my sun sign, causing me to feel more self-possessed with the light of my inner being.

Garnet - A stone of vitality and dreams, garnet increases the flow of the body's natural energy systems and helps them to function effectively. Relating to the mysteries of sex and regeneration, garnet is a stimulant that connects us to our deepest memories. Garnet used in deep magick calls upon the dreaming self to invigorate our astral bodies which results in the clear memory of astral travel and dreams.

Hematite - Hematite is best known for its ability to be a gentle grounding stone. It's often placed near the lower parts of the body (feet or ankles) to act as an anchor when working strong planetary magick. Hematite is composed of oxidized iron ore and has the ability to carry magnetism. Because of this, hematite is often used for both drawing and release. A great stone to use in meditation and sitting practice, hematite will help you let go of any extraneous thoughts that just won't seem to leave your brain when you want them to. Whereas other grounding stones can almost be too grounding, hematite is flexible and seems to know exactly the right level of grounding you need to have at one time before "shutting off."

Iron - Iron is extremely protective and has the ability to ward off any type of curse or spiritual malevolence. In fact, some believe it can even ward off all "supernatural" beings including those of the faerie world. Because of this, iron is considered to be obnoxious and offensive to the fae. Some historic lore claims that iron was used as a defense against Witches. I find this interesting as ancient Witches were probably very likely to use iron *for* magick. Iron nails are used in coffins and their use in American folk magick traditions like hoodoo is well known.

I include iron here primarily for its classical associations with Witchcraft but also as a practical means. Working deep magick can sometimes mean that unsavory people will be attracted to you. There will sometimes be times that you feel the need to protect yourself against the malevolent magick of others. For this, iron is an ideal tool in the art of psychic and magickal defense.

Jade - Jade is a serenity stone and is excellent for healing illnesses associated with stress and feelings of overwhelming obligation. The modern Witch tends to be quite busy and I find that jade helps to bring me back into my physical body so I can make sure I'm taking proper care of it. When you want to re-enter your physical body to reduce stress without being overly grounded, jade is a great choice. A wonderful ally in healing others, jade is a good stone for folks who are beginner healers or want to give their healing practice a nice little boost.

Jasper - Both grounding and stabilizing, jasper is a fantastic stone to use when doing any sort of earth magick. If this chapter on the earth had an official stone sponsor, it would be jasper. As a stabilizer, jasper has the interesting ability of taking control of wild and unfocused energy. This makes it a great stone to use while conducting ritual with large numbers of people or one that has many beginners. Without grounding down the energy that you want to "send up", jasper will form an appropriate container to focus the energy long enough to get sent out.

Jet - Think of jet in Witchcraft as the sister stone to amber. Like amber, it is not an actual "stone" (rather, a form of coal called lignite) and can generate electrical charges when rubbed against wool or silk. Jet is receptive and draws powerful energy, while amber projects it outwards once it's in your grasp. Jet has the ability to both repel negative energy and to transmute it into productive energy depending on how you program it.

Lapis - To be honest, lapis lazuli is my favorite stone and I usually give it vast amounts of praise that I won't give too much of here. Lapis is an ancient stone and its use is easily traced back to both Mesopotamian and Egyptian cultures. As a stone of great power, lapis should be worn with care if you're unfamiliar with its spiritually as it can turn you into a channel for big amounts of energy to flow through. This is the reason why it's beloved by psychics and mediums. To the Witch, lapis helps us focus our energy and amplify it when we're sending it off to a specific goal.

Sacred both to Isis and Inanna, lapis has always associated itself with the major ruling goddesses of the ancient world. In looking at the descent myth of Inanna, you'll see that a strand of lapis beads was one of the beloved vestments she had to surrender when approaching the gates of the dead. Because of its associations with Underworld descent, lapis is good to wear during the dark times of the year or times when you're exploring the shadow side of the soul and the gods.

Malachite - Malachite is a stone of alignment and is good to use in the journey towards self-possession and autonomy. Stone practitioners tend to warn against wearing malachite as it is seen as the "mirror of the soul." Lore states that wearing the stone will reflect in the physical whatever exists within the emotional (positive or negative). I'm not sure if I fully agree with this, but I use malachite in short workings to align my soul with my physical body. If this stone had a mantra, it would be "I AM."

Merlinite - As you could probably guess from the name, merlinite is useful for amplifying all forms of magick. Though I don't often come across merlinite, I've always thought that it would make an excellent point to a wand or other such energy-directing tool. Merlinite can assist the Witch with summoning up the powers of the Mighty Dead and opening to channels for spirit communication in ritual.

Moldavite - Another "new age" stone, moldavite can elevate the consciousness and activate the higher self within any person. Used for dimensional travel and assistance with ascension magick, moldavite aids in all things relating to the higher spiritual planes. Moldavite paired with merlinite would combine the magicks of both the old and new age and would make a fabulous rotating beaded necklace for any magick worker.

Moonstone - Long considered a stone of the Goddess in all her forms, moonstone is sacred to all things lunar and celestial. Following the lunar associations, moonstone is excellent for someone interested in honing the intuition and improving their natural psychic abilities. Highly associated with the goddess Diana, moonstone can be a conduit to call upon this Witch-goddess in times of need or adoration. Moonstone is a stone of wishes and I use it when working goal magick. When contemplating the nature of your work in the world, moonstone can be used to gain perspective and clarity. It's like looking at your own personal world from the distance of the moon. Possibly overwhelming while on the earth, but manageable from the distance of the moon. Moonstone has a gentle nature and promotes kindness and peace.

Obsidian - Obsidian is fierce, protective and is associated with all dark goddesses such as Hecate and the Morrighan. A stone of the shadow mysteries, obsidian unlocks the unconsciousness and makes room for the shadow self to come forth and speak. Obsidian is a favorite material for scrying and some of the most beautiful scrying mirrors I've ever seen have been made from it. With its reflective qualities, obsidian challenges us to look deep within to the hidden places that we love, fear, or have yet to discover. Though there are many types of obsidian with their own special qualities, nearly all forms have something relating to "vision". It's because of this that I use obsidian to look past the "mess" of a situation to its true core. Divinatory stones made from obsidian are excellent to use before working a spell to foresee the possible outcomes.

Onyx, Black - Onyx is another grounding stone and has the ability to easily manipulate negative energy. When programmed for protection, onyx will immediately banish malicious intentions that cross the path of the wearer. However, onyx can also direct evil energies and is sometimes employed for hexing and cursing. Never accept an onyx stone from someone you don't know or don't trust. If you have been hexed, have no fear! Onyx is a strength-giver and can supplement depleted energies that have been wrongfully taken from you. In a more practical sense, Witches can use onyx to find rest after an exhaustive working.

Opal - Opal is a stone of beauty and is good to work with to appreciate the beautiful unfolding of the divine universe. Opal contains all the colors of the other stones and can be an amplifier to all other stone energy. Some lore states that opal is unlucky, but I find this to be mostly nonsense. Opal only brings misfortune to those who deserve it, as it speeds up the karma of whoever wears it. On the other hand, ancient Roman lore states that opal is extremely lucky and serves to stimulate luck and a positive outlook. Opals, like humans, need water to grow effectively. This causes opal to be associated with humanity and reminds the Witch to be charitable in her work and to work towards the benefit of all people.

Quartz - Probably the most common stone used today, quartz is an all-purpose stone that really is a jack of all trades. Like opal, it is an amplifier that will increase the power of any working you do. Different colors of quartz have their own unique properties: Rose Quartz - Used for all matters of love, rose quartz opens the heart center and causes a gentle warming of the emotional body. Rose quartz is probably the best stone to use for self-love and to increase feelings of personal worth in the world. Smokey Quartz - This is a manifestation stone and helps seeded projects come into fruition. Charge a smoky quartz when doing magick on the new moon and watch as your work rapidly comes into being before the moon turns full. Rutilated Quartz - Heals the soul and causes the regeneration of damaged soul pieces. Rutilated quartz is a great ally for someone who is struggling to bring down the "I Am" for the goal of personal autonomy. Wear rutilated quartz to integrate all parts of your being into a healthy, holistic whole. Tourmilated Quartz - Also a great amplifier, tourmilated quartz brings luck and success to any endeavor. It is particularly useful in clearing away unhealthy energy patterns and promoting balance. Ruby - Also related to the mysteries of the blood, ruby aids in strengthening and refining the natural abilities you were born with. Another stone of immense power, ruby is worn to stimulate pure life force energy and its spirit is a great ally to any magick worker.

Serpentine - Serpentine contains all the powers of the snake totem and gifts the Witch the powers of wisdom and regeneration. Use serpentine in your work when petitioning the gods for cunning and adaptability.

Tiger's Eye - The emphasis of pure bravery, tiger's eye allows us to do what needs to be done regardless of any would-be obstacles that we might face. It erases doubt and empowers us to fulfill our Great Work without the fear of failure holding us back.

Topaz - Topaz is an envisioning stone and helps you see to the core of any matter. I consider topaz to be a stone that well defines a true Witch; one who is courageous, a visionary, and filled with purpose.

The Mineral Kingdom makes working with the earth element both fun and challenging. If you feel overwhelmed by all the stones out there, try picking up one that looks prettiest to you. Seriously, that's what I did at first and I now know a whole host of stones I work with in my daily practice. If you find yourself particularly attracted to one stone, chances are high that it's a stone you're meant to be working with.

When forming a relationship with a stone spirit, it is best to approach it while in a deeply grounded place. Your chances of success at forming contact are more likely when you're operating on a similarly low vibration.

Stones can also be paired with certain herbs to charge the stone and increase its natural potential. This blending of energies is part of the fun of working with natural materials in Witchcraft and really helps to keep the Craft interesting for long-term practitioners who don't want their work to become boring or rote.

Like the energy of the element itself, working with earth requires both patience and persistence. Forming a good relationship with earth leads to mastery with all other elements. The wisdom earth provides is an absolutely essential quality of an empowered Witch. Without wisdom, we really are a shell of what we have the potential to become. With wisdom comes the skill to apply knowledge and the resourcefulness to use that knowledge for the betterment of our lives and others.

Chapter 5

Spirit

I am convinced that there are universal currents of divine thought vibrating the ether everywhere and that any who can feel these vibrations is inspired.
- Richard Wagner

Spirit is the final element and the one that completes the five sacred points of the Witch's pentacle. Spirit is the paradoxal element, existing both within and without form all at the same time. It is for this reason that spirit can easily be considered the most mysterious element.

What exactly is spirit and what form does it take? That's part of the paradox and also the argument. In substance, we can think of spirit as the texture of the other four; wet, dry, arid and earthen all at the same time. It is the reaction that's generated within your being when you experience those elements, lightly or with depth. Spirit in form is basically comprised of all things we might have a hard time describing with the five physical senses, even though it is all things physical as well.

In its non-physical form, spirit is the force that surrounds and animates all cells within the cosmos. It is electrons, neutrons, and the tiniest invisible particles that animate them. It has been called the "God Particle". Spirit is the area of metaphysics where everything gets tricky. This is where science raises its skeptical eyebrow and claims that because it cannot be "recorded" by any quantitative measures, it doesn't exist. For this reason, many people find developing a relationship with spirit to be one of the most difficult parts of their practice in Witchcraft. What does this result in? A shallow understanding of the nature of spirit, where it comes from, and how to best come into conversation with it. In reality. Spirit isn't any harder to touch than the other elements. We just have to go at it with a slightly different approach.

In China, spirit is known as qi (chi) and is a vital concept in all areas of traditional medicine, dance, food, fighting, loving and even breathing. Spirit is both seen as innate (yuan qi) and acquired (qi) throughout the course of one's life. What is interesting is how the view of qi is acquired. The consumption of food, the movement of breath, and the stimulation of the body in exercise all result in the positive accumulation of qi. I mention this because it shows that although spirit appears to be non-physical, the image of invisibility is entirely an illusion. Spirit flows in accordance with both physical things and non-physical things. The movement of the breath for example is a physical action that is accompanied with an energetic reaction in the mind. Spirit is the composite relationship of both experiences.

Spirit within each element

Spirit is unique in that it plays a specific role within each of the other elements. Knowing how spirit interacts with the other four helps us to know how to effectively summon up the other elements, and how to strengthen our connection with spirit itself.

While working with the other elements in your practice more deeply, it will become easy to see how each supports the other. Once again, the idea of spirit being separate from matter is an illusion. Focusing on how they are intrinsically connected helps to affirm their connection together.

Spirit: Air – The power of chi that circulates through the breath. The sending of life-force power to the higher self through an upward shot of breath. Spirit's ability to expand and live within all places. When using its Greek name of Aether, it is the air that the gods and immortals breathe.

Spirit: Fire – Catalyst. The spark of creation from which all energy emerges. The metabolism within the body that consumes food and converts it into energy. This is the "inner fire" that burns within the earth of humanity. The purpose-driven existence.

Spirit: Water – Survival and the origins of life. Spirit's ability to flow, nurture, and sustain. The mysteries of shaping and molding magick in all its forms.

Spirit: Earth – Beginning, return and all things in between. The mysteries of hibernation, slumber, and source. Spirit in earth reminds us of the paradox of individualism. Though we each have a unique body, we are all a part of the interconnected root system of our planet.

Spirit and the heart

We've already discussed water as an elemental associated with love. Love exists within spirit but on a whole other level. While water is the emotional side of love, spirit is divine love and the enactment of that love in all the worlds.

We say that spirit is the heart of things because it is the ultimate point of origin. According to the occult Principle of Mentalism, everything you experience is a reflection of the divine mind. This is not to say that you don't have your own unique ideas, but simply that the spark of that idea had its source in spirit, in the center.

Many cultures believe that the core of the soul resides within the heart. Though I'm not sure I believe that myself, it does show the intimate connection that heart and soul share together. Spirit is not the same as the soul. The soul contains spirit, but is a little more complex than spirit itself. When we speak of spirit on its own, we speak of the purest stuff of creation.

Spirit in ritual

It seems like nearly all Traditional Witchcraft rituals I've partici-pated in worked with spirit on its own in some way, while that number is about half and half for Wiccan rituals. The number drops significantly when talking about pan-Pagan rituals in general. I have a few sociological theories for why this is but I'll save that for another time.

When spirit is called in circle, it is usually done within the context of the direction "center." What do we mean when we say center as a direction? Well really, center isn't exactly a direction. It is the "magnetic north" of your own internal compass and the hand that holds it. Because spirit is the point of origin, center is the anchor that brings connection and activation to everything else.

Spirit is often omitted in the directional quarter calls because center isn't often thought of as a direction. In the tradition I was trained in, we definitely did not call spirit center on its own. It was almost assumed that spirit was there by the power of our presence. While it is certainly true that spirit resides where the Witch resides, there is still value in calling spirit out on its own.

The word "namaste" comes to mind. Often used in Hindu rites and even in yoga, namaste roughly means "the divine in me acknowledges the divine in you." This is part of what happens when we call spirit on its own. We are acknowledging the divine presence within every person and every element. This is a sanctifying act and if the space was not blessed before the calling of spirit, it most certainly is now.

The "weapon" of spirit is the altar pentacle, the symbol that weaves the five elements together in perfect harmony. It is usually placed within the center of the altar, once again displaying its association to the center direction. While the other elements/directions are often called by the raising of arms to each direction, spirit is usually called by having the spirit summoner place their hands on the altar pentacle, focusing on the binding together of each element.

In my own coven, spirit is called by "gathering" together each element and "tying" them into the center. The simple act of connecting them together is what calls spirit into place.

Family, beyond blood

Spirit is the featured element of concern to the family mentality and all that comes with it. For good or bad, family is something that can never be taken from us, even in death. Though a family might grow and change over time, or one may not even seem to have one to begin with, it will always emerge as long as spirit runs through it.

Spirit is the invisible blood that connects family where genetics lack. Where I grew up in the south, we call someone kin when they're family, even if they're not related. When someone is kin, it means they're family by spirit. The bonds of spirit, once established, can never be broken by outside influence. A summoner of spirit infuses their being with the element. It doesn't just "go away" when you're tired of its presence.

Recognizing the connection between spirit and kin can be highly valuable for the strong formation and sustenance of a coven. Though all covens go through natural stages of growth (as Judy Harrow calls them: forming, storming and norming), anchoring the bonds of a coven in spirit ensure that the divine reflection of each individual is honored throughout the process.

Creatures of spirit

You could probably guess that the creatures of spirit are, well, spirits! There is no being in this world or the others that are not comprised of spirit. Every elemental of earth, air, fire, and water is also made up of the stuff of spirit.

It can be argued that even those elementals who correspond to one of the "core four" elements are still primarily spirit, due to their typically invisible natures. This again leads us to a great question to ponder: What ratio or percentage is spirit to matter, in both elementals and beings of tangible form? Honestly, I can only wonder. In terms of the bodies of humans, I feel that spirit is always present and the force of its presence is entirely up to the commitment and will of the person who is cultivating that connection.

That said, I believe the form of the human beyond death is primarily spirit, though maintains a connection with each of the "four core" elements. It is this connection to the four that allows the discarnate human spirit to return to Earth and to reincarnate when it chooses to. If a spirit did not have any sort of connection to the material elements, it would be difficult or impossible for it to establish a link or anchor in the physical world. If you follow this idea, then it's reasonable to suggest that such a spirit would not be able to be reborn into a physical body. From this one point is very clear, connection with each element is vital for survival and growth.

Summoning spirit

We already touched upon the most common way spirit is approached in circle, but let's unpack that a little further. Calling spirit for any working can be quite simple or highly complicated. Personally, I'm one for theatrics (I'm a Leo, go figure) so my callings tend to be a bit flashy. I'll go over different methods to suit each taste.

In its simplest form, summoning spirit consists of finding center and breathing in pure life force energy into that center. Then, the life force energy of the center expands outwards to encompass all directions and all areas around you. That's it.

From that method, you can start to get creative. You might take those breaths into the center, but also add in "gathering" arm motions like you're pulling invisible things towards you from all directions and placing them into the center of the circle or working space. You might then quickly trace a pentacle at each direction (including above and below), and use those sigils to "hold" the gathered spirit matter in place. If you have ever performed the Kabbalistic Lesser Banishing Ritual of the Pentagram, this is essentially what is happening. And if you're ever even in the presence of that rite while it's being performed, you're likely to be familiar with how tangible the presence of spirit is once its complete.

With the altar pentacle being the weapon of spirit, I often like to take up this tool with both hands and hold it close to my chest while calling the fifth element. As I do this, I imagine the pentacle forming a mini portal of sorts, opening the way for energy to flow in. As I lower the pentacle before me onto the altar, I sense the settling of the fifth element into my space. I take a sharp breath in, a sharp breath out, and it is done.

Ritual for spirit connection

To commune with the element of spirit, we will use both the core of our inner selves, and imagery from the outside world. To engage in communion with spirit, we must remember that it flows both from inside our center, and towards our center from the "external" universe. This ebb and flow is how spirit exists inside and outside of both time and space, all at once.

Because of these factors, communing especially with spirit when you're not used to it might leave you feeling flushed with a large influx of energy. This is normal and can even be an exhilarating experience for someone who could use a little boost in their personal energy reserves. If you find it's too much, simply use any of the simple or expanded grounding techniques we covered in our earth lessons.

Before you begin, you can set up an altar that includes the typical spirit correspondences. You can use associations that are both traditional and ones that you have come across while developing your own relationship with spirit. Here are some of my own personal associations with spirit:

Purple and violet colors
Many-pointed Stars
Spirals
Clear Quartz and Amethyst Crystals

LED lights
Altar Pentacle
Photos of beloved dead
Vesica Pisces symbols

Once the altar is set, you'll want to get into a very light meditative state. Shallow but concentrated breaths for a count of around four will do. As you meditate, begin to open up the mind to the idea of what spirit means. Begin to sense where it might be flowing from. Do you feel the gentle tugging that might pull you forwards or back? Is it a tingling sensation in the core or the crown of the head? Perhaps an increased psychic awareness? These are all experiences that tend to follow the invocation of spirit. Simply focusing on it already begins the process of inviting its presence. It has already begun to join you.

Now we'll begin our focused effort to engage spirit to the best of our abilities. When ready, take up the wand if you have one or use the tips of your fingers to cast a spirit circle around your space. You probably have your own way of imagining the circle power but I'd like to challenge you to really pay attention to this particular process. The circle is cast with spirit and it is spirit that is primarily responsible for keeping it together. If you imagine a gentle line of electric energy being laid down upon the circumference, imagine it instead as being like an atomic blast of fierce and thick energy, pouring out from the Otherworld. As the line is drawn, this energy is also filling the inside of the circle. Your space is being filled with a huge amount of power just while casting the circle. This is the type of power that is not typically called upon until the raising of energy later on in a ritual.

Let this energy coalesce and swirl about you. Breathe it in and let it trickle and mingle with all your bodies, physical and etheric. Then speak the words of communion:

Out of the void, out of the black

Spirit emerges on the breath of the gods
From the center and from the core
Coming from nothing and coming from all

From the hallowed spaces
and the twilight realms
Neither this nor that
But all things combined

The great quintessence stirs
The stars display their majesty
From the four, the one is born
and on the edge we dance

Spirit of all, be with me now
Settle here in the circle of the arts
For between the worlds we stand
And this work is blessed by our union

The light grows brighter and thicker as it increases its pace around you, then settles down with the slowing of your breath. Be within this place, feeling the settling of spirit and the senses that come with it. You can sit within the presence of spirit until it grounds down on its own, or you can channel it into a token for future use. I like to draw up the extra energy into the tip of my wand. When there is still spirit essence about I can continue to swipe the wand about until the air is back at its neutral state.

When working with spirit, it is important to remember that energy at its core is entirely neutral. It is the nature of the person working with it that determines the nature of its course. It is because of this that spirit is the element that challenges us to determine that "weight of our worth" and our place in the cosmos. Do you choose to stand in only one world, or within them all?

Chapter 6

The Gods

Love is the joy of the good, the wonder of the wise, the amazement of the gods.
- Plato

The image of a Goddess or multiple goddesses is something that is nearly always equated with the image of modern practitioners of Witchcraft today. Though these views may be muddled and filled with confusion, one thing is certain; the feminine divine is a power that for our religious culture is here to stay.

In my initial studies in the Witchcraft traditions, I learned of the Goddess and came into relationship with her through a very Wiccan worldview. She was consort and guide to the God in his journeys, one half of the great coin that makes up godhood. She was all things sweet and lovely while the God was all things wise and strong. So many people today hold this very common dualistic belief where female-based theology is concerned.

For many years I shared this view until the image of the Goddess began to change for me. In my studies of the ancient lore and Traditional Witchcraft schools of thought, she began to encompass more than I ever thought imaginable. No longer was she just the creatrix of all things sweet and lovely. She became a fierce warrior queen and a dark crone who dances at the gates of the Underworld. She became both what I thought of as feminine and what I thought of as masculine all at the same time. This slightly androgynous and all-encompassing vision is one I still hold today.

Discussing our vision of the gods in any way can be a touchy subject. No one wants to get the impression that their view of the divine is wrong or skewed in any way. When this occurs, it can bring about feelings of inadequacy and doubt. "If the gods are not how I envisioned them for the past twenty years, how are they even real at all?" Questions like these arise when we forget the panentheistic nature of the Witch's religion. For if the gods exist within all things, then certainly they can be all things to all people. Debate that occurs outside of the joy of pluralistic conversation distracts us from remembering our direct connection to the forces that are responsible for our lives and deaths.

As I mentioned already, my view of the Goddess has morphed frequently throughout my life. The images I see of her seem so clear I can touch them, yet later turn into symbolic keys for me to dive deeper. It is important to know that while she can be all things to all people, that doesn't mean she must always be as she seems. What you desire in her - the warm, comforting guardian- may not be how she will come to you when you need the fierce challenger. When we surrender in a way to the realization that her very existence defines the mysteries of the cosmos, we can better understand how to develop that relationship.

This journey of continued understanding and partnership is not an easy one. It requires us to ask important questions about the spark of the divine within our own lives. As the Maiden of Light, she brings illumination to the hidden caverns of the Witch's heart. Are you ready to have all things in your being become visible? As the Crone of Shadows, she challenges us to face the most dreadful pains and fears that we so often like to push down. She places the blade of liberty before us, if only we have the courage to sever the ties that bind. These can all be experiences of both pain and beauty, yet each one will mold our spirits, deepen our connection, and transform our lives. Through the Goddess, we can truly claim our power and own our place in the world.

Who is the Goddess

When looking at the lore of the Witch we find many fascinating writings of the Goddess of Witches all around the world. Somewhere between all the differences and similarities, we come to a core understanding of what the Goddess may have meant to the Witches of old and what she could mean to Witches today. From Goddesses of battle and death to goddesses of flowers and rainbows, she seems to have a place amongst all things in the world.

Some of the oldest artistic icons we have of a goddess figure come from the areas around France where we have an icon that is called Venus of Willendorf. This busty and fruitful goddess shows off large round hips and exaggerated breasts, suggesting that she was seen as a fertility deity. Goddess as giver of life is a common idea, especially for ancient peoples who relied upon the gods to push the cycle of the year forward to ensure the survival of tribes from the harshness of winter. To these people, the Goddess of fertility was savior mother and savior both. A light in an often difficult world.

As old as the fertility goddess, we also find the crone, warrior, and gatekeeper goddesses. To modern people, the image of gods of death doesn't often sound very savory, but to the ancient peoples who respected the cycles of life and death, she was a welcoming hand and a relief from suffering. We see this in Athena, goddess of wisdom and war who protected the city of Athens from the constant threat of outside invaders. We see this in The Morrighan who gives us the strength we need to stand up and claim a firm place in the world. Where we are stubborn and slow to change, this goddess gives us a sword we think is too heavy. We clumsily lug it around not sure what we do with it. She keeps saying "pick it up, keep trying, pick it up." Eventually we do pick up the sword and feel how it becomes an extension of our own arm. We feel the power of our will becoming sharp and agile. And of course, the Goddess knew we could do it all along.

Some Witches and general followers of earth-based spirituality see Goddess as Gaia, the living breathing Earth beneath our feet, and that is all. They don't believe that there is a separate stellar being in the skies. The gods are in the here and now within all things physical. Some scientists hold a view similar to this (though often without the God part) and use this "Gaia Theory" to explain how all things on Earth are connected through the multitudes of ecosystem processes. In a way, holding just this view makes it almost a secular form of Goddess reverence, if such a thing exists.

These are just a few samplings of the vast archetypes the Goddess has been given over time. Entire books have been written about this topic and will continue to be. What I want us to explore is our relationship to Goddess in any form. We explore this in many ways. By seeing where we fit in the archetypes, by researching, by devotion, and by action we can begin to understand the incredible mystery we call God Herself.

Gaian energy

The Witch calls upon the energy of Gaia to fuel her magick from the external realms. As we learned in our lessons on Earth, the power that runs through Earth is dense and nurturing. Another vibration of energy exists within earth that is both earthen and divine. Gaian energy is the life blood of Goddess manifest in the physical. This is again a paradox, for there really is no separation between the physical and divine other than what the senses perceive. Buzzing at a higher vibration than earth energy, Gaian is like "earth of spirit" and animates the flow of earth power with the intelligence of Goddess-mind.

Gaian energy is the reflection of the Divine Mind as seen in the earth below our feet. It is part of what comprises the natural ley lines that gird the globe and make up the patterns that form the etheric body of earth itself. Yes, Earth itself has its own etheric body, physical body, and divine body. Most Witches will work with physical earth in various forms, but working with this etheric energy gives us a few great advantages. First, working with Gaian energy helps to stimulate it and get it flowing. Getting it moving will actually nurture and heal the physical part of earth. So working with Gaia then becomes a natural healing mechanism for the planet. That's as green as Green Magick gets. Second, while physical earth energy is so dense that it can often ground us when we do not desire to be grounded, Gaian energy will provide the energy we need and will allow us to hum in vibration with whatever type of energy is required for the Work we're doing.

Gaian energy is cool and refreshing. It's also strong. It's like plunging your face into a cold waterfall after a hot hike through a mountain path. The water beads against your face in a refreshing sting.

The symbol of Gaian energy is the rose. The symbol of The Lady in all her guises, the rose holds the beautiful spiral of infinity within its bud. It also holds the thorns of the Warrior Queen and the roots of the Crone that sustain it. The rose takes up the power of the Earth and transforms it to a living being of beauty and grace in the physical world.

She who is maiden, mother, and crone

Popular in Wiccan theology is the idea of a Triple Goddess that many of us are familiar with. Here we find what seems like three simple archetypes: maiden, mother, and crone. Like many triple deities throughout history, we find descriptions of each that change and flow in different directions depending on the adherent. I'll give my take on how I perceive this force to be.

As the Maiden, we find the sweet, pure, essence of spring. She is the laughter in the greening woods that drifts upon the warm spring air. She is the creative force that melts the frost and warms up the soil for the newly emerging plant life to spring forth. She is innocence personified. But do not be fooled by her sweet demeanor. For the Maiden also embodies trickery, chaos, and the "curiosity that killed the cat." Some see the Maiden as similar to the queen of the faerie realms. She will invite you for a fun walk through the woods, but you might lose track of time and realize you don't know your way back to the mortals' world. When we approach the Maiden, we must do so with integrity and the purity of a simple heart.

Many are quick to think of the tale of Persephone's capture by Hades to the Underworld as an example of the perils of Maiden power. Sometimes having the face of one who is young and in control is exactly what can make one the target of danger. It is for this reason that the Craft is known for rituals to bless and protect young people as they age. As they age and come into a great position of power, the container they have to hold it in must also expand. So she is ever expanding, ever growing, and ever dancing.

The vision of youth is much like the rose so revered in the Witchcraft teachings of old. It is slowly growing at first, climbing and coiling up the trellis following the growth of its sister plants. But one day, it veers off and stems its own path. Once day, a bud forms and blossoms into the fullness of color and fragrance. And then almost as if in an instant, it is gone. Wilted, withered, and falling to the soil. It is this impermanence that gives us appreciation for youth when we have it. It is what grants hope to elders, for when they look at youth, they can see the potential for all that could be.

We can also look at the cherry blossom as another symbol from the lore of plants that personify the maiden. Where I live in Washington DC, cherry blossoms reign supreme. Given as a gift to us from the Japanese, they only bloom for a couple weeks out of the entire year in the spring. When they're in bloom, all of the district is transformed into a fabulous display of pink, white, and red. All sacred colors of the Goddess as maiden. When it's time for the parade, dancers roam the street dressed as colored flowers and all sorts of fantastical creatures. Though it may be unintentional, this whole observance seems very much to be in reverence to the young Maiden, ever so perfect yet ever so impermanent.

The next personification is Goddess as the Mother. Perhaps the most recognizable of the phases, the Mother is exactly what she sounds like. She is the life giver and the great nurturer of all things. In her light aspect, she heals the sick and is concerned with the bounty and blessings of all things bright and lovely. In her dark aspect, she is a fierce protectress of her children. She is the lybris wielding Goddess of Crete, so revered by the Minoan civilization. As the middle personification, she stands between the young one and the old one. In this role she is the great balancer and it is she who all seers must approach to look forwards or back.

To the Witch, the Mother is the mover of energy. She is the "mover and shaker" of the Goddess aspects and we look to her to get things done. In her lunar form she is the full moon, the time when the moon is most visible in the sky from the vantage point of Earth. On the full moon, people who never pay attention to the moon usually at least give it a glance. This makes sense because the Mother commands a respect about her that none can deny. With that respect comes compassion and the desire to do what is right. Ever-moving and ever concerned with the next approaching phases, she tells us to prepare for our work and to stand grounded in the present.

There are many symbols associated with the Mother that we all know so well. The image of Isis suckling baby Horus or even the older images of the fertile and large-breasted Venus of Willendorf. I've often wondered why Goddess as Mother seems to be the most commonly displayed Goddess personification in ancient art. It's likely that this phase was viewed as the "height of life" by many, but I'd bet that it's more than that. What mysteries does the Mother hold? Each of her symbols is like a facet on a bright diamond and could all be explored in full depth on their own.

When I think of the Mother I like to think of the birch tree so beloved by both the Celts and the Norse. Called beith by the Celts, the birch was a purification tree and the wood of cleansing and new beginnings. For the Maiden is not the only one who has the chance to be reborn anew. When we approach the Mother phase, whether woman or man, we all have a chance to cleanse, purify and re-dedicate our intentions. Each phase of life holds the microcosm of all other phases within its eye.

Finally, we come to the Crone. Although it seems that most Goddess aspects are that of the Mother, there is no other image better associated with the Witch than the Crone. Most defamed throughout the ages, words like "Crone" and "Hag" are often used as insults to describe someone who is old and ugly. This is more of the old patriarchal attempt to strip away women's power and Witches' power. After all, the Crone is the most powerful of all, having gained all the wisdom of the years within her aging body.

The Crone is the village wise woman, the healer and teacher of all teachers. None move forward without first seeking her council. None can properly prepare to pass through the gates of death and rebirth without first taking her hand. It is she who holds the key to the mysteries beyond what we can grasp with the hand of mortal flesh. It is for this reason that some fear her, thinking her a vengeful spirit who rides the wind cackling and looking for souls. Certainly she can be, as we see in the Welsh goddess Cailleach.

Crone goddesses are often associated with Witchcraft in some way. One of the most revered of all Witch goddesses would certainly be the triple goddess Hecate. Although not seen by the ancient people as a Crone (she was actually more of a beautiful Maiden), she seems to be a special case in that she has grown into and accepted the new role by her new era of adherents. Hecate holds the symbols of illumination and secrets in the dark; key, torch, knife, lantern, snake. Her image is the waning or dark moon, when the powers of night unfold in all their suspicion and wonder.

Relationship of the Goddess and the witch

To the Witch, the gods are not distant vague beings. They are not beings of remote worship to be looked upon in fear or contempt. Rather, they are beings who require a fluid and moving relationship with us. Though these relationships will be unique and changing to every Witch, there are a few things we can keep in mind in trying to build a fruitful relationship.

Worship - Worship is one of those tough words to bring up in discussion around Pagans. It's also one of those really fun words to bring up around Pagans, especially when a bunch are seated around a big festival fire. "Worship" brings up images of adherents bowing down in supplication yelling "I'm not worthy!" For some paths this is true, but for the Witch this could not be further from the truth. Worship to me means that I am recognizing that there is something far greater than myself, beyond what I can perceive. But that is not to say that I am not a part of that greater whole.

By acknowledging the greatness and brilliance of the powers I'm working with, I also acknowledge the greatness of my own power. When we look at it in this way, worship becomes a mutually beneficial process for the Witch and the gods. We gain greater appreciation for our own gifts. When all powers are a reflection of the powers of the divine mind, all things are brought into the fold in the worship process.

Gathering at the moons is usually thought of as the traditional way to give worship to the Goddess. Even though we can do it at any time, there is something special and powerful about having these times marked out and set aside. Looking up at a big bright full moon and blowing a kiss to Goddess can be a simple yet powerful act of worship.

Gratitude - We've already gone over gratitude extensively. Giving thanks can certainly be considered an aspect of worship. Again, we acknowledge the gifts of the divine and the magick of existing in our lives. Gratitude for the gods doesn't mean we're never allowed to be angry. If we find ourselves in turmoil or deep loss, it is natural to feel confusion or even anger at the gods. "How could you allow this to happen?" you might ask. When we experience times like this, the practice of active gratitude that was built up over time will serve as a type of emotional padding to see you through. The harshness of loss might not burn so hot for so long. Sorrows can become a little less sorrowful. When these feelings are felt, our understanding of the gifts of Goddess can only grow.

Stewardship - When I speak of stewardship, I'm specifically referring to acts of taking care of the planet and helping the many beings who live upon it. It is my firm belief that Goddess wants all people to have the resources they need to live happy and successful lives. She wants us to take care of the environment, animals, and fellow humans. When we engage in acts that support this type of work, we're making a statement to the gods that we want to further the progress of the things that they brought into creation. Volunteer, perform activism, or lend someone a helping hand. By being good stewards, we co-create a better future for ourselves with the gods.

Communication - The foundation of any good relationship is open communication. This means meditation, prayer, and devotional ritual. It can also mean speaking with the gods at the most "mundane" times like taking out the trash or washing dishes. Speaking to the gods directly in these ways opens the way for deep communication over the long term. Remember too that communication also means actively listening. Make time for silent (in mind and speech) meditation and open up to what the gods and spirits have to say. Communication must always go both ways.

Research - There are many wonderful books totally dedicated to the stories of Goddesses from all over the world. Not only do they tell the ancient myths, but many also follow the history of Goddess worship around the globe. Knowing Her stories makes you a part of them. Pagans today are reviving the worship of the Great Mother and it's good to know where we've been to glance at where we might be heading.

I suggest picking a goddess who you might not be very familiar with. Read her myths and learn about the people of the culture she's part of. You might even make an altar in her honor or design a special ritual. Learn as much as you can about the Goddess in all her forms. You never know how she might present herself to you.

Observing Earth Cycles - Practice the wheel of the year, but also the times in between. There might be a favorite tree in front of your home. What does it look like in January? How does it begin to change once the air warms up a bit? When do the first leaves start falling? The Goddess speaks to us in the cycles of the seasons in both large ways and small. Remember, we are not separate from the Earth. When the environment around us changes, something changes within us too. When we observe the changes around us, we follow the gentle pulling that leads in the direction of the divine.

Other than celebrating the major sabbat feast days with traditional ritual, here are some other ideas for observing Earth cycles in a way that will bring connection with Goddess:

Plant a garden or even take care of one single plant. Develop a relationship with that plant spirit and ask it how it's changing at the start or end of each month. Visit an orchard and go apple picking if you can. Orchards are sacred to many gods and are tied to some of the most intimate myths and legends revolving around the change of seasons. Take a bite of an apple and raise your class to Pomona, the orchard goddess in the spring. Sip some cider in the fall and send a prayer to Demeter in thanks of a successful harvest. Keep track of when the sun rises or sets each day and center your daily sitting practices around those times. Take note of how your practice feels at different times of the year in this way. Do you feel greater connection when the sun rises earlier or later? I'm not a morning person by any means but waking up when the sun rises early helps fuel my day with strength and energy. Seasonal Altars - If you have a general permanent altar, consider keeping up with the turning of the wheel by adding some seasonal flare. A few fall leaves once they start falling in your yard, or perhaps a few cut tulips once they start popping up in late winter. It doesn't have to be anything elaborate, but if you're the creative type this can be a really fun way to honor the Earth Mother throughout the year. Daily practice and sitting in a dedicated place is my preferred time to spend quality time with Goddess. When I approach her grounded and centered, all my channels of communication can become open and welcoming for connection.

Gifts of the Goddess

For the Witch to develop a deep relationship with Goddess, she must understand the many ways in which Goddess gifts us, seen and unseen. When we start to look at this topic, we can begin to realize our full magickal potential as priests and priestesses of the Goddess.

Gifts of the Goddess given to the Witches are so widely discussed that every Witch will probably give a different answer, a different list. Before we discuss the powers in detail, we must first explore one question: where do the powers come from? Obviously we could say they come from God Herself, the gods, and the cosmos as a whole. But have you ever stopped to wonder who exactly is responsible for dishing them out? In medieval magick, we see that old grimoires speak of various spirit agents who are responsible for gifting a sorcerer with different powers. In the grimoire known as The Ars Goetia (the first section of the Lesser Key of Solomon), we find descriptions of various spirits that can be evoked through sets of seals by the magician. This technique is mirrored frequently throughout many of the famous medieval grimoires such as the Book of Abramelin the Mage.

More information about medieval grimoires and ceremonial magicks can be found in some of the books listed in the bibliography.

Next, there is the natural world to consider. Would Goddess instruct the rocks and trees to give the Witch her power? One could also argue that as the entire natural world is part of God Herself, both the trees and Goddess directly are involved in the blessing of powers. If we believe that Goddess lives in all things, then it would make sense that the powers would somehow originate from her in some form or another.

In all of the complex questions that arise from the "what is the source of Her powers" question, a certain paradox is present: the powers within God Herself are also the powers that are naturally present within us all. Whether she is giving us powers or awakening them within us is mostly irrelevant. What matters most is in knowing that we have that divine spark within us and so we will encourage it to rise. The following ritual will call upon the Powers of the Goddess to align you to them.

Exercise - Ritual to awaken the powers of Goddess connection

Materials: Any combination of three or more of the herbs-vervain, mugwort, willow, acacia, primrose, rose, orris, wormwood, lotus, myrrh, heather, rowan, or violet. High proof alcohol (rubbing alcohol is fine if it's high enough). Cauldron. A token to use as a talisman (pendant, stone, something travel-size). As early before this ritual as possible (a week is preferable but a day or two would suffice), grind your herb combination into a powder and mix it into your alcohol base. We're making a magickal fluid condenser. The easiest way I've found to do this is to put the mix in a mason jar and give it a good shake every day. This will dissolve the herb powder into the alcohol so you get a nice even burn.

Plan the time to be on some holy day. A full moon or within

the days leading up to one would be ideal for this. The time doesn't matter, though I prefer the hour between 11:00 p.m. to midnight when working with raw Goddess powers. This liminal time between the days makes for a smooth transfer of energy.

Create the circle space as you normally would. Pour the fluid into the cauldron ahead of time before you enter your trance state. You will want the fluid to burn for around 5-10 minutes so just small splashes will do. If you've never burned a fluid condenser before, you might be surprised how far just a little bit will go. Have the chosen talisman present on the altar as well.

After you enter a light trance state by whatever desired means, begin doing a thorough cleansing of yourself and your altar space. You are becoming a vessel for the Goddess to bestow the holy powers of the Witch. As a vessel, you must be ritually "clean" for the power to pass and settle properly. To really ensure a smooth passage, you could even fast the day before the rite is performed. Don't forget to cleanse the chosen amulet token.

At the height of the light trance state begin a kind of ecstatic swaying, either back and forth or in small circles. Here we're using movement to open the way for divine connection and the conference of power. Begin to intone words to call down the presence of the Mother to your circle. You can say anything that comes to you in the state of trance, or something like this:

Lady of the moonlit round
I call you to this space
What I seek you have made found
within this hallowed place
Mother of the cauldron flame
arise and make your presence known
Reveal to me your blessed name
and join me in my home

Carefully set fire to the cauldron and gaze within the depths of the growing flames. As the flames lick and nip at the air before you, feel the essence of that fire encircle you and twist around your being. Feel the warmth of this energy as it coalesces around you and enters your blood stream. You might even encourage this process by intoning the vibration of vowel sounds low in your throat. This is another trance induction technique that encourages the rising of primal life force energy. What do you feel? What do you see? What powers does the Lady gift you with this night?

Tap the chosen talisman three times either with the tips of your finger or with your wand. Allow the energy flowing about you to enter the talisman, creating a vortex within it, a mini cone of power. Allow the energy of the vortex to settle and calm down a bit. Continue to breath and allow the cauldron flames to continue burning if they still are. This time allows the power to "set-in" before you get up to end the rite.

After a time you feel is sufficient, ground down excess energy and then place the talisman on your body somewhere. If the cauldron flames have not yet gone out on their own, you can put them out now by cutting off its oxygen with the cauldron lid or some other flame-proof top. Keep it on you at all times, at least for the first day or two if it all possible. The work is done.

Goddess as warrior

Women today are just starting to reclaim in greater numbers the image of woman as warrior. This isn't a new idea. In so many ancient cultures we see women who took up roles of defense within a community. The Roman Empire, South Asia, India, Indonesia, Persia, Syria, France, and countless tribes in Africa all featured female warriors. Some of them, like Joan of Arc, have made history for their bravery and skill in battle. In cultures like these, female strength was recognized as a useful and important power.

We see this especially in the possibly-mythic nation of female warriors called the Amazons, from Greek lore. The lore from ancient Greco-Roman art and literature suggests that the Amazons were based around Turkey and at one point conquered all of Asia Minor. Believed to be a focal point of their worship was Greek goddess Artemis, who rules over not only the spirit of war, but also agriculture, hunting, children, animals, and the moon. Art depicting Artemis with her bow and hunting hounds at her side very much resemble ancient art depicting Amazonian women. Did the Amazons inspire the artistic images of Artemis, or was it the other way round? More likely is the concept that both modes of representation were intertwined as a general archetype of woman as warrior.

In the Goddess as warrior, we find an interesting spectrum of personas and actions depending on the culture of the people. In some instances we find her as quite frightening, a symbol of a being who strikes fear in the hearts of her enemies. Hindu images of Kali can appear quite intimidating at first glance, covered in blood and dancing on a corpse, adorned with bones as jewelry. To one who does not know Goddess in this way, it seems odd to give praise to such a figure. But the Warrior Queen is a fruitful ally, inviting us to face our fears and pick up the swords of our various battles when we need to. When we experience injustice she calls out to us: "Rise up! Defend yourself!" In other ways we see goddesses such as Athena, a war/wisdom goddess whose power often lies in the wisdom to pick battles appropriately, finding peaceable discourses or actions whenever possible. She tells us that although it is ok to defend ourselves, we must never enter battles without seeking the wisdom of differing opinions.

Take a strong breath this moment and ask yourself "in what ways does the Warrior Goddess speak to me?" I like to do this while gently gripping the hilt of my athame, tuning into the power of will and the knife's edge. Is she telling you to take immediate action? Perhaps she wants you to just sit with yourself and observe your goals and aspirations. What tasks do you still need to accomplish that sometimes feel like an uphill battle? Why does it feel that way? When we attune with the Warrior Goddess, we can identify the parts of ourselves that need to take up the sword, or to just sit and listen. This view of Goddess speaks to resistance and the power required to push back.

Goddess as healer

One of the prime duties of the Witch is to bring healing and comfort to his community. The role of the Witch as healer is seen widely across folklore, myth, and oral tradition in many places around the world. In times past, there was little separation between the spiritual and the physical in terms of medicine, and the Witch knew how to talk to both worlds and use the healing forces of both to her advantage.

Goddess as healer is an image that many Witches find they easily connect with on a multitude of levels. When most people think of the healing Goddess, they think of benevolent and gentle figures such as Brigit. Brigit, who hails from Ireland, is one of the most famous goddesses of healing and she is most certainly revered as such by many people all over the world. So much so, that she was one of the deities who was turned into a saint by the Catholic church during the time when the church was seeking to eliminate or convert the great Pagan icons (including the gods themselves). With Brigit we find a goddess who travels the lands in search of ways to heal and assist the sick and afflicted. I often think of Brigit as a sort of female Christ, wandering around in search of further ways to be of service. I connect well with this image as it is part of what drew me to study the Craft in the first place. The call of the Witch is a call to a path of healing, both for yourself and those around you.

Deeply seeking the lady

If you take nothing else away from this chapter, take away the reminder that we must never let our relationship with the gods of our choice become stagnant. The gods are not dead and they listen and speak to us in ways both large and small each and every day. Through continuing to learn, practice, and study under the many guises of the Lady, we learn to master our Craft through the very hand that birthed these powers to begin with. The God.

Although god images are closely aligned with the Witch as much as goddess images, the ways they are connected to the Craft are often entirely different. This difference in presentation throughout the past few centuries has done a great deal to shape one's relationship with the masculine divine, for better or worse.

In the most extreme negative, we find the god of Witches presented as a devil from the time of the inquisitions and the reign of the Church of England. Looking at the various woodcuts from the time will show this devil as a beast with horns and cloven feet, presenting a black book for the soulless denizens of Hell to sign. He is seen as wild yet cunning, using the skills of deception and seduction to lure weak women and men into a life of sinful servitude. In the Renaissance era we see that image shift. The God of Witches becomes less nefarious and more of a romantic symbol for the mysterious allure of the wooded places becoming less and less inhabited by the "civilized" people of the age. If we look closely, we can see the survival of the God in Pan, Dionysus, and the other gods from what we now call the "classical era." Flash forward to the mid-1900s and the resurgence of Paganism in many forms. While the Goddess mostly stays the same, the God once again shifts into a more prominent role upon being adopted into the Wiccan mythos by Gerald Gardner. There becomes a dualistic approach to the gods here, with (in many traditions) the Goddess still appearing slightly "above" her male counterpart. Of course, there were people who taught a much different approach at these times such as Victor and Cora Anderson of the Feri tradition. In ecstatic traditions such as theirs, the God took on a more gender-neutral or softer tone than the God of Wicca. In any case, we see the blossoming of the God who begins to be celebrated in just as many forms and names as the Goddess. This is still happening in this present year as many Witches and Pagans continue to push themselves beyond the traditional views of what the goddesses and gods of our paths should or shouldn't be. The God will likely continue his role as the transformer, adapting himself into whatever image he needs to while still remaining strong in the heart of the Witches.

Who is the God

Many books on Wicca and Witchcraft today would spend this time discussing the ways in which the God is everything that is the opposite of the Goddess. They would say that while the Goddess is all things lunar and cool, the God is all things solar and hot. I wonder what would happen if we challenged these preconceived ideals early on? What if beginner Witches were taught to approach the God as a wild, unknowable mystery, someone to be courted and sought after through deep reflection and personal exploration? We can approach the God with the academic approach that we do with Goddess, but we must also take into account that the God of Witches is an untamed energy that cannot be easily explained by a book or even through the lectures of a well-seasoned Craft teacher. The mysteries of the God must be explored through tangible interaction and personal experience just as much (if not more) than through symbol and word. We keep this in mind any time we seek a deeper under-standing of the God.

Triple God - poet, father and sage

Although the Goddess has held firm in the triple aspects of maiden, mother and crone, the God's "faces" are a bit more various and don't always have much to do with sage. The system I favor gives the God a triple role of poet, father, and age which

I feel nicely highlights the main imagery in the Witch's God.

As poet, the God is the young and innocent personification of everything new. The first budding leaves on the spring trees are brought about by his touch. He is Jack in the Green, the young Green Man who exemplifies the spirit of all nature in its purest, most raw form. Those in the Feri tradition might call him the Blue God, he who is the soft carrier of the black heart of innocence. He carries the spirit of the song and dance to those who gather for Pagan festivals, his scent being the newly-kindled fire and the sweat of the drummers. I call him the poet in this aspect because the young god speaks through the creative heart and is drawn to all things bright and beautiful, in whatever form they take. The poet God is the muse that inspires all new magick to blossom forth from the hearth of the Witch. As the father, he is the teacher of lessons both esoteric and worldly. Many Witches who come from oppressive Judeo-Christian sects can have trouble connecting to this aspect of the God. While he does have a stern side in this aspect, his compassion and tender heart make him more approachable than you might think. The father watches as we make mistakes and occasionally lends a hand to intervene, but will more often challenge us to come up with solutions on our own. He is the reason why the Witch values the quality of personal responsibility so highly. God as father grants us the tools and resources necessary to claim our power and live the life of our dreams. His face is seen in all the gods of leadership such as Zeus, Jupiter, and Ra. In the manifestation of nature, he is the lush, dark forest on the edge of summer and autumn. As the sage, the God is the wizardly grandfather figure, the wise cunning man at the edge of the village. He rules over the sacred transition of all things that prepare for the arrival of death. Although his imagery can make him appear elderly and feeble, do not be fooled. There is still great strength in the things he influences and we would do well to not dismiss it. The sage God is the great recorder of time who charts the progress of the Earth and the stars throughout all the ages. Like the Crone, he is the welcoming relief of death after a life well-lived. He brings us the rewards of memory of regeneration at the time of harvest.

Relationship of the God and the witch

The connection formed between the God and the Witch is often different in many ways from the relationship forged with the Goddess. While the Goddess' connection seems to be easily forged through the work of ritual and prayer, the God seems to ask for a little more in some ways. Throughout the course of writing this book I spoke with many Witches regarding their personal connection to the masculine divine. I wanted to know if it was similar to the feminine and if not, what exactly made it different. Of course the answers were many and varied (ask three Witches one question and get six answers), the common thread seemed to live within the way the God communicates and responds. The Witches I spoke with mentioned that while Goddess messages will often come in the form of personal insight, dreams, or visions, God messages arise from gut instinct, reactive emotion, and day dreams. This intrigued me because the way many Witches are taught to form relationships with the gods are often quite similar in nature. Yet here we find these very different and unique standards being put forth by what feels to the Witches like God Himself. When we reach out to the old, wild gods, we are usually first met with pure and simple energy. The energy of the masculine divine on first approach feels blissfully uncomplicated, untethered. Even if we have not approached the Witch's God before, we find a strangely familiar feeling, like the embrace of a long-departed friend we never knew we missed at all. That feeling soon changes as he begins to play with those deep and hidden places in your soul, calling them so for the hope of reuniting them. The experience of unifying the dark and light places within us can be both joyful and terrifying (sometimes both at once, strangely enough) so the

Witch's relationship with the God requires a certain level of understanding before deep magickal work can be engaged in. In this unifying challenger-aspect, he is the Baphomet, the merging of what looks on the surface to be opposites yet work together beautifully together to form a working whole. On Baphomet's body is written *solve et colagula*, a hint to the process the magick-worker must go through to achieve such union. A relationship must be formed with yourself and God Himself at the same time. In particular, the God of the Witches is brought into focus when we engage in activities that are known to describe his common nature: Taking Risks – The God is brave but not arrogant. Like Athena, his bravery is laced with heavy influences of wisdom and calculated response. We take risks every day that either lead to our advancement, or our demise. Which path do you choose to take today? The definition of risk always involves the possibility of losing something. But the risks we take that are infused with the wisdom and bravery of the divine put us in a greater position for advancement and gain rather than loss. Visiting Wild Places – In the wild hunt, the Lord of Death races through the forest with his hounds collecting souls estranged from their bodies. The wild places are also where Pan makes his home and encountering him there can mean either madness or bliss. Visiting the wild places helps us remember our origin. The wild places strike a chord of primal yearning to return to simpler ways. They strip off the façade of class and status and demand we reach for more. Being in the Body – The God is in many ways both mortal and immortal. In the great wheel of life, we see him going through the cycles of life and death that we as humans are also subjected to. This is not the God showing some kind of weakness, but a reminder that we can still be powerful and holy while present within our physical bodies. Being in the body means we take care to keep ourselves healthy and fit to the best of our abilities. We eat good food and move around. Whether you have a large body type or a small one, the God only requires that we have strength to the best of our abilities. Physical strength can lead to less struggle when we expand the core of magickal practice. Having a strong container means I can hold more than if I did not. Communication – We cover communication in this book frequently. The value of keeping our words in good order and in a place of truth can never be understated. The God as sage and scribe places strong value in words and thought. Having our daily communications with others and the gods, we remain connected to the True Will which means greater connection with God Himself. Just as with Goddess, we can more closely align ourselves with the God by taking time to learn his other popular roles: God as Psychopomp – This is the role of Hermes and Mercury. As psychopomp, he acts as a guide between the worlds to both other gods and mortal people alike. Hermes is thought to be one of the very few gods who can pass freely through the gates of the Underworld without negative repercussion. This role is similar to Hecate, who first informed Demeter that her daughter's captor was none other than the king of the Underworld himself. God as psychopomp acts as an intermediary between the Witch and the unknown places. I take this to mean the unknown places within each of us, in addition to the external realms. When we form a relationship with this god, we become masters of traversing the realms of spirit and form. God as Trickster – This is the role of gods like Loki, Coyote, and even Set. On the surface, he is often tasked to take on a role that sometimes seems diabolical even to the one being tricked. Loki certainly gets a bad rap on a cursory glance in these stories, always appearing to set the other gods back a step. But the role of the trickster is still an important one. Tricksters are the necessary boundaries set in place for us to measure our true potential. They challenge us to bring more of our skills and heart to the table. Trickster brings out the problem-solver in us all and can help lead us to a better understanding of our own innate power. He also challenges us to not take ourselves too seriously all the time, which in itself is a great value for all effective magick-workers to have. God as Healer – There are clearly just as many healing gods throughout the world as there are healing goddesses. One of the most important gifts in the ancient world (and still in the modern world) is the ability to heal and be healed. In the God, we find Asclepius who is considered the father god of medicine. Although not an Olympian, his role to the emerging physicians of the time cannot be understated. As the god rules over the natural elements, he is responsible for the herbs and elixirs that make up the Witch's potions and remedies. Death Dealer – In his most misunderstood and feared role, the God stands at the gateway of death. As an aspect of his face as the sage, he is the sometimes-frightening transformation required for things to begin anew. We find this in the "Charge of the Dark God" where he says "I am the laughter at the edge of death." The death dealer is only frightening to those who don't fully understand the mysteries of resurrection. All that's born is born to die, and all that lives has an existence beyond what we consider to be the world of the living. Accepting this grants us liberation from the constraints of rigid materialism.

Exercise - Aspecting the Many-Faced God

Spend a fair amount of time researching the many roles of the God. Does one appeal to you more than another at this specific point in your life? Which roles feel similar to those held by the Goddess and which feel different? Which form are you hesitant to approach and why? Although personally my relationship with the masculine divine is in a very early evolutionary stage, I still take time to work with these various energies and at least ponder the role they play in my life and magick. While we can become familiar with the Many-Faced God through research and reflection, the God requires a more visceral understanding. He wants us to feel his presence in our guts and bones. For that to happen, we must aspect. If you're unfamiliar with aspecting deity, see the next chapter on ritual and read up a bit on it first. To aspect the Many-Faced God, we'll use the power of masks. Masks are tools that don't seem to be used much in Witchcraft ritual anymore outside of sabbat celebrations, but their power and effectiveness is a true gem in the magickal toolbox. We all wear masks both energetic and emotional every day. They help us discern what role we're playing at any given time. In large public ritual, I wear the mask of the High Priest, connected and confident. In my day job, I wear the mask of the well-read nerd, the go-to guy for any number of office projects. By using energetic masks, we can call the different faces of the God to our being. Being "in his shoes" in this way gives us an opportunity to deepen our connection with him for any work moving forward.

Enter a trance state and begin to think about the work you did in learning about the many roles of the God. As you fall deeper into the trance state, pick one role and concentrate it within the palms of your hands, forming a mask. Place the mask over your face and take in the presence of what that feels like. What is your immediate reaction along with the reaction of keeping it on for several long moments at a time?

Pushed by intuition, you might feel called to integrate that mask fully into your spirit for a time. Do this by pushing the energy of that mask all the way into the head. Merge fully with the God-role you've chosen. You can let this presence "take over" for a time while still maintaining consciousness. Maintaining consciousness is important so you can look back on the experience later and reflect on how it went.

Obviously this work is best performed by those who have a really good grasp at grounding and centering. Both of those practices are required for being able to aspect the God effectively. Being able to take on the face of the God and remain anchored in the natural world (his domain) can be one of the most effective ritual actions the Witch can engage in.

In conclusion

When I teach introductory Witchcraft classes and the topic of the gods comes up, there are some definite starting points. We learn about them and what they do. We begin to forge relationships and establish connections that are meaningful for us and them. What's interesting is when connection to the god comes up as a topic outside of the introductory courses. It's interesting because so often the same questions come up. People want to know what others do to connect to this mysterious power we call "the gods." They want to know how to strengthen these relationships and bring them into the fold of their daily lives. This tells me that no matter where we are in our practice, we all crave that intimate relationship with the unmanifest divine. Working with elements and the spirits is part of that, and working with them directly in ritual is another part. Having a multichannel approach helps us to come to the work of divine connection with a sense of commitment and grace.

Chapter 7

Deep Ritual in Witchcraft

Witchcraft is so connected with ritual that they're nearly an inseparable pair in the literature of Witches both non-fictional and fictional alike. So deep is this connection that some people might go so far as to only connect Witches with strange rituals at midnight, perhaps in the forest under a full moon. This is one of those cases where the stories can quite actually be true! Witchcraft can very much be about ritual and so often it comprises a large part of a Witch's spiritual and craft practice.

Simply put, ritual as described by scholars is any set of actions that are performed in a particular order with some kind of intention. With this definition in mind, a great number of things we do every day without thinking of them could easily be considered ritualistic. Brushing your teeth, tying your shoes, and even checking your email at a certain time in the day could all be considered forms of mundane ritual. They have intention. This differentiates ritual from habit, where the person is almost not thinking about what they're doing. Biting your nails isn't a ritual, it's a habit. If however you insist on waiting until 10pm when you're sitting on the sofa in your living room to bite your nails, those circumstances could then be considered ritual.

There are as many types of rituals as there are Witches, and every Witch usually has loads of them written down in personal books or stored in the depths of the memory. Even rituals that are traditional morph and change over time. Many people experience a great ritual and try to adapt it for their own. Even if they try to get every aspect of the ritual down, some parts of it will inevitably change. Some people even go to a ritual that absolutely inspires them to the core and change it to make it even better. In either scenario, the ritual changes based on the Witch writing and performing it. What I want to discuss here is how we can shape and change our rituals to be the most effective and transformative as we progress.

Identifying the types of ritual that the Witch is likely to engage in will help us get a clear image of the true range of ritual an experienced Witch leader is likely to be approached with as their practice deepens. This is especially true for the Witch as a religious leader who will be called upon by the community to perform any number of observatory or transformational rites.

Rites of passage

These rituals designed to mark the next stage in a person's life can be surprisingly simple, to highly elaborate depending on the ceremony. Handfastings (wedding rituals) and Coming of Age rituals tend to be the most elaborate while Graduation and Pet Crossing rituals are often the most simple. In any case, these rituals tend to be about something other than the person leading the ritual. The ritual leader in this case is the intermediary who facilitates the movement of the spirits and the transference of blessings.

A commonality with group rites of passage is that they are often not engaging enough for the audience. Think of the typical funeral. A priest stands over the casket and recites lyrics by rote while everyone clusters around each other and mourns. In this case, the rite is serving the same use as someone mourning on their own in private. If we were to make a funeral rite deeper, we would look to see how we could engage the participants. It is not just the spirit we are honoring at a crossing, but also the living people who they leave behind. After all, death is harder on the living than it is on the dead.

Rites of passage where one person is the focus (Coming of Age rituals) is another story. Rituals like this are often begun with a period of seclusion, followed by a transformational process and a community honoring. The effective ritual here would be one that focuses on blessing what is already a natural passage, and links the person into the community they are joining. When someone comes of age in any way, the generation they are becoming a part of changes with them. The spirit of the age is shaped by what they contribute. Therefore, the community's engagement should be taken into consideration.

Sabbats, Esbats and holy days

When we get into holidays, the mixed bag of rituals we get will get even more mixed. Generally, sabbat rituals are often observatory and many Witches don't think to include any deep transformational work within them. However, some do! This is where it gets odd. Have you ever noticed that sabbats like Samhain, Yule, and Mabon tend to include deep transformational work while the rest of them end up being observatory? I've attended sabbat rituals up and down the east coast and abroad for years and I still see this trend.

What if all our holiday rituals were observatory and transformational, all at the same time? It is possible if we think of the many factors that go into creating a powerful sabbat ritual. It isn't hard to do these either. Every sabbat and moon date holds immense power with it that will aid us in this process if only we call upon it.

Devotional ritual

Although there is a devotional aspect to all rituals (or there should be), there are types of rituals that are simply meant to honor the gods, give thanks, or commune. I mentioned that sabbat rituals often just end up being observatory (a type of devotional) which I hope did not give the impression that I think ritual for observation or devotion is meaningless. On the contrary, some of the most heartfelt ritual I've ever done was for devotion.

Though some people don't like the idea of "worshipping" the

gods (they say it sounds too Judeo-Christian), practicing devotion to one's deity is something that Pagans have done since the dawn of time. The reason that devotion ritual has survived so long is that something really powerful is born from them. For one, the practitioner is growing their relationship with the gods or spirits when they engage in this practice. The other is that it makes you take notice of the fact that we are so small, yet so connected to the greatness of the cosmos. Devotional ritual makes us pay attention.

Deep devotional ritual means that we're not just falling to our knees and throwing our arms up in praise (though sometimes my love of the gods makes me do that!). Depth occurs when we realize that we are devoted to the gods and the spirits of the land because they are devoted to US. Recognizing that reciprocal view of human and spirit is the first step. The second is layering. When I layer devotional ritual, I add many facets to it to ensure that it is engaging and transformational in the process. Devotional ritual should change us and make us even more devoted than we were when we started. The main theme of your ritual might be to offer gratitude, but you might also add on a layer of heart blessing, to ensure that your awareness of this powerful feeling of gratitude sticks around and increases. Layering these rituals will make them more meaningful for the devotee and the center of the devotee's attention.

Ecstatic

You may think that ecstatic ritual is more of an adjective to describe ritual that is wild and unbound by conventional rules. If you think that, you're partly correct, although there is so much more to it. When we are in ecstasy in a religious sense, we are letting the wind take us where it would. This is the realm of trance, dance, and all things that spring from the deepest caverns of the heart.

Religious ecstasy is deeply rooted in multiple faith traditions.

Even Evangelical Christianity has its "caught up in the Holy Spirit" experiences that could be considered a moment of ecstatic ritual. It is good to note though that the ecstatic ritual goer does not lose consciousness when in these moments. Rather, they are hyper-aware of everything that is going on, often across several realms. This is the shamanic experience of being the gatekeeper between the worlds. The ecstatic worker is opening the way for the spirits to come through and sing within the hearts of those in the circle. This is not possession, but rather self-possession. It seeks to open up all the channels that are usually closed in other forms of ritual.

The beauty of ecstatic ritual is that is can be performed for the most meaningful of reasons, or for absolutely no reason at all. Consider the drum circle. I've been to a great many drum circles and they sometimes have an energy raising "goal" that is being worked towards. But more often than not, the goal here is to simply be in the company of others and to let the powers of the beat and its energy move you. It's like therapy for the soul. More serious forms can be found in trance breath work where the practitioner must work hard and with focus to achieve the state they need through breath, chant and intensive visualization.

Magickal goals

I'm sure some will disagree with me here since many view ritual for magickal goals as just doing spellwork, but bear with me here. When we really look into it, you might think a little differently about spellcraft's relation to ritual.

We most commonly think of spells as a component or agenda item in ritual and it often is. We often set up entire rituals to house a spell. Housing spells with good ritual is one of the first things we learn how to do when learning effective spellcraft. It gives the spell a good foundation to spring from and contains the energy in a way that's solid and focused. The ritual becomes the container that gives the spell a container which then allows it to collect more power before it's ready to be sent out into the world.

Housing spells with ritual is always great, but what if we centered our entire ritual on the spell itself? Think of it this way. If I'm doing a spell for prosperity, are the other elements of my ritual contributing to this? I might cast a circle with lush green energy representing prosperity and abundance. In my calls to the elements and the spirits, I can address them with a specific request to join my circle in the spirit of abundance. I might wear ritual garb that's deep purple to correspond with Jupiter, the planet of the abundance. While centering, I would call prosperity to my center. When grounding after, I would ground out all poverty thoughts and take in all the abundance of Earth. I could go on but you get the picture. Framing ritual to center entirely around our goals takes a little extra planning but the boost you get from it is definitely worth it in my eyes.

Oracular

Most things using the term "oracular" tend to be used in conjunction with things like divination or scrying. However, for our use we can think of it as any type of word that is focused on direct speech with the divine. Oracular can be ecstatic, but not always. Oracular can be devotional, but not always. What is important here is not so much the goal of what you're trying to do when speaking to the gods or spirits, but rather the method in which you do it.

Delphi, Greece, is most famous for its history as an oracular site. The Oracle at Delphi was dedicated as a temple to Apollo and was also connected with the worship of Gaia. The priestesses were called the Pythia and were responsible for the operation of this temple's function as well as the visual performances given to the pilgrims who would visit the site. The oracle likely had huge influence throughout this part of the ancient world and people would come from far and wide to listen to prophecy and receive direct speech from the gods. Above the temple were carved words from the now-famous Delphic maxim, "Know Thyself." This was the challenge of the pilgrims who would visit. Apollo is the god of illumination who would speak through the oracles, but it was seen as an insight from the divine speaking from within the reader. The oracle was consulted for everything from personal matters to issues of war and state. This wasn't just divination, it was direct consultation with the gods.

Aspecting is a practice based on the possession of a priest or priestess by a spirit or god. When possession occurs, the other participants of a circle can speak with the spirit or god and engage in direct verbal communication with them. This is much different to ecstatic ritual where everyone is totally aware of what they're doing. Although the priestess is delivering the speech of the gods, they will often awaken with having absolutely no memory of the message they presented to the rest of the circle. I have seen this happen many times and I can assure you that this experience can be very legitimate and very real. I have seen quiet and mousy priests turn into something like a mighty and thundering king. I've seen priestesses who aspect a goddess and tell me things that they could not possible know on their own. This impressive form of oracular ritual is extremely intense, but something that I think everyone should experience, even if occasionally. Speaking with a priestess who is aspecting a deity can bring incredible insight, even on things you had no idea you needed insight on in the first place!

Other forms of oracular ritual consist of summoning a spirit or requesting the presence of a god and listening to how they might manifest in a certain setting. As cheesy as it sounds, the Victorian table tipping séance is a classic example of group oracular ritual (when it's done for more than entertainment of course.) We can do our own solitary oracular ritual by adjusting our scrying practice and making a ritual surrounding that. The goal of the scrying procedure then steers away from seeking information and turns into an open form of clear communication between the ritualist and the divine.

Avoiding rote ritual

No one likes going to a public ritual that is generic and typical. We've all been to them. Rituals where the leaders call the quarters with the same mechanical scripts, light candles like robots, and read liturgy like they're reading a refrigerator repair manual. We all start learning ritual like this primarily because it is safe. Performing the same motions over and over gives us practice and helps us to develop a good foundation to stand on when we hopefully start doing more moving ritual later on. The problem is, so many of us don't move on past this point. We keep the safety net because we're afraid of messing up or afraid of going deeper. And that's the key word here, fear. As we all know, fear is the type of resistance that wants to keep us stagnant and unchanging. When we don't move forward in our ritual practice, we miss out on the opportunity to become more powerful in our craft. Fear can be a great motivator when we see it as a challenge to rise up and meet, but when fear manifests in ritual planning, the outcome is usually rote, stale ritual that leaves us feeling bland and indifferent.

What are we risking? Perhaps we fear summoning powers we think we cannot control. Maybe we're nervous about messing up and making mistakes. These are the most common stories we tell ourselves that keep us from performing our best ritual. Who cares if we mess up? Ritual is organic and comes from the inspiration of the divine mind. The divine mind has some order to it, but it is more often messy and wild. We get caught up in the "stuff" and the performance of it all. Putting on a good ritual play can be wonderful, but not if it leaves you feeling unengaged and unmoved. When we look at what holds us back when it comes to ritual, we will find that the big risks we're nervous about making are not so big at all.

When we get down to it, there are only a handful of blocks

that keep experienced practitioners from moving past rote ritual. In particular:

Seemingly Limited Options: "I've never seen it done any other way. This is the only way I know." Not a great excuse. Witchcraft requires continual learning so why not learn other ways to do something? You won't learn how someone else invokes differently than you until you ask them. Ask multiple people, learn why they do things, and explain why you do what you do. This will result in asking yourself why you do what you do. Those questions we ask ourselves form the internal dialog that causes the shift we need to speed up the learning process. A good book resource for expanding the knowledge of ritual options is "RitualCraft" by Amber K and Azrael Arynn K (Llewellyn 2006).

Fear of Public Embarrassment: No one likes the feeling of getting something wrong in front of a group of people. That's the ego trying to shape us and make us better, which is fine, but it doesn't have to rule us. Fear of making a mistake in ritual is what causes public ritualists to always "keep it simple." For the record, I have been to some amazing rituals that were quite simple in their layout but had profound effects on me. Simple ritual done with intention rather than as a result of fear are totally different things.

A priestess I know here in Washington DC puts on some of the most touching and deeply moving sabbat rituals I've ever attended. They usually consist of tools like a bowl, water, knife, apple, or other things you could find in a common kitchen. They usually don't last longer than twenty minutes and there is no complicated motions or potions involved. She directs ritual by shaping how our spirits experience what is right in front of us. The small bowl turns into a fabulous bubbling cauldron. The apple turns into a magickal wishing apple that contains all our hopes and desires. She doesn't worry about impressing an audience with her simple tools because she has the confidence in knowing that she's going to move people. When we remember that performing public ritual is a selfless act of service to people and the gods, then making a mistake becomes less important. In turn, it becomes less important to the people who are experiencing ritual with you as well.

Poor Planning: I tend to procrastinate with some things as I know many of us do. But planning ritual shouldn't be one of those things. Whether it's for yourself or a whole group of people, having effective ritual is a part of our spiritual practice in Witchcraft and is something we should devote an appropriate amount of time to. We all lead busy lives and l often catch myself giving the excuse of "oh I don't have time to do X". If these focal rites within your practice are not enough to be warranted a good span of planning time, then what does deserve your attention? Ritual that is rushed and planned in the heat of a panicked moment (especially if you're not versed in ecstatic ritual) will show as such to others.

I should also mention that ritual shouldn't be too planned out to the point where you're devoting the length of time to it that someone would need to write a dissertation. If the problem is that you feel stuck and that's why it's taking so long, ask for help! Collaborating in ritual planning is an extremely rewarding practice that can result in some beautiful and transformative experiences.

Not thinking outside the box or reaching past comfort levels: It can be hard to think of ritual that is creatively engaging when you sit down at the computer or with a pad of paper and a pen. Forming interesting ritual ideas that keep us and others guessing is the result of pulling ideas from multiple sources. If you take ritual ideas from other rituals you've been to, try looking at other rituals that you might not view as so sacred. There is a specific way my neighbor plants her tulip bulbs in the fall. She lays them all out in circles around her and plants each one in seemingly random patterns. In the spring when they pop up, the formation is beautiful and you would have never guessed it by seeing the planting process. Things like that give me ritual ideas. Always be open to sources of inspiration.

Along the same line as not thinking outside the box is doing ritual that we think is "safe" or "comfortable." I've got news for you...no ritual should be safe! Let me unpack that a little though. This is not to say that ritual has to be dangerous in any way. Rather, it should be something that pulls us beyond the boundaries we put up for ourselves that prevent us from coming into our full and radiant potential. Feeling nervous about going where no ritual has ever gone before? Good! Like anything in Witchcraft, facing a challenge with bravery in the face of risk is a process that births true power and transformation.

The elements of deep ritual

We are trained at the start of our studies to follow a formula-based approach to ritual consisting of a set of parts that often changes only slightly. This is tradition and there is nothing wrong with that. Wiccan Witches in particular hold close to this formula and there usually isn't much variation. I'm raising my hand here, guilty as charged. It took me a while to notice that "breaking the rules" and stepping outside the standard formula would often result in some very interesting ritual. Traditionally, the formula I'm speaking of consists of ten parts:

Cleansing and clearing space. Cleansing and clearing people Casting the circle. Calling the quarters/elements. Invoking deity. Perming the ritual's working or observance. Cakes and Ale. Thanking deity. "Dismissing" the quarters/elements. Opening the circle. I should say that this formula has existed in Gardner's time for a reason, it certainly works. But like any other system, holding onto it too tightly can result in the development of co-dependence. Yes, we can become co-dependent on a ritual formula. It's safe, it's simple, and it means we only have to worry about step number six in this case. You can follow the outlines above, but thinking that you have to follow the outline above to perform deep ritual is where the trouble arises.

If we look at the formula above and break the ritual outline down into some rearranged categories, we get a new formula that allows for greater creativity and pushes the boundaries of what you might be used to doing. The traditional ten steps might all be within the new formula, but are likely to be changed significantly if we don't become slaves to it. The system I use cuts the ten steps in half and leaves us with this:

Deep Witchcraft Ritual Formula. Create your world. Shift consciousness. Summon powers. Direct and seal. Engage the hearts, minds, and wills of all involved with every step of the above.

Create your world

Clearing and setting up space could fall under here, but this step leaves room for so much more. The environment of ritual (especially for groups) is important. When we set up the space we have to think about the physical space and the energetic space. What does the space look like to the beings of the otherworld? I call this "creating the world" because it points to the importance of creating an entirely new reality for the environment you're working in. Magick is often met with some big hurdles before it can manifest in the physical world. When we perform magick, we are tampering with the very fabric of our reality and all realities beyond it. Magick taps into the limitless possible outcomes that can occur in our lives and "pulls down" the reality we desire. In the Qabalistic sense, it is the journey from Kether to Malkuth. Because of this it is important that we create a world for our ritual that is suitable to doing this type of work.

When looking around at your physical space, what do you see? Is there clutter or mess? Technological distractions? Lighting distractions? Creating effective physical space engages the creative brain and helps to send the signal that something important is about to occur. When in doubt, I like to take a minimalist approach. Personally, I feel like too much stuff in a room causes too much distraction and can keep your physical selves from the appropriate focus needed to do your work. There are occasions though were minimalism is exactly what you don't want. Here are some examples of how altering a physical space can change a ritual environment.

Tabitha is hosting a Samhain ritual in her living room. She has a lot of furniture so she just pushes it to the sides of the walls. The shift in furniture puts emphasis on the dusty television top in the corner of the room. The furniture's displacement makes her feel stressed out because she knows she'll have to move it all back herself later. It makes the room feel rushed and artificial. At the last minute she decides to put everything back and switch up what's there. She drapes black sheets over everything and places dead branches from outside behind the covered couch and television. The room is filled with black curious shapes and foliage that gives the feeling of a deeply wooded cave. Tabitha altered the environment with some simple tools that will be easy to clean up right after.

Star is hosting a baby blessing in the great hall of a Unitarian Universalist church. Four walls, nothing else. The space feels hollow except for the chairs of the audience and the altar at the center. She wants it to feel like a real temple so she erects several altars at all the focal points of the room with flamboyant cloth and brightly burning candles. She covers the windows with fabric gauze that keeps the room well lit but creates variations of the lighting. Star hangs streamers in a pattern at the door that creates a hallway effect. When the guests enter, they know they are entering sacred space.

Stella is performing a solitary dark moon ritual in her new apartment in the center of midtown Manhattan. Car horns screech and partying tourists shout from outside. Artificial light from the street lamps flood in through her big bay windows. Stella knows that the contemplation required by the dark moon could be reached more easily if she shut that stuff out. She covers the windows with heavy blankets or blackout curtains that keep any light from seeping through. She turns of all appliances that generate light and even puts a towel in front of her apartment door to keep the hallway light from coming in. Everything becomes pitch black besides the glow of her altar candles. There's nothing she can do about the noise outside, so she gets some earplugs from the local convenience store, or maybe some noise cancelling headphones with her favorite melodic tunes. Her urban quarters become a solemn fortress for total focus and concentration. Once the physical considerations of the space are taken care of, we can begin to think about the invisible forces that shape the environment. There are so many things that are happening in the invisible world around us and it wouldn't do us well to stress out about all of them, but there are a few things we can take into consideration when forming the energetic aspect of our world.

Spirits and beings of the area: Is there an earthbound human spirit who tends to cause trouble? Perhaps your ritual area is near a graveyard or place of power with active spiritual presences. Find a way to speak to the beings. You might even set up a pre-ritual to form an agreement that spirits who aid your work are welcome to the environment. Other considerations would include summoning beings like the Lare who watch over the activity of homes. Human-created vibrations: This would include radio waves and other electromagnetic frequencies that we cannot see. I suggest forming a matrix web around your area to block out these energies. Quartz crystals with their points facing outwards create a grid of energy around a space that does well to block out this type of interference. Some people even bury stones or other objects around their homes to set up a permanent type of system. Onyx or hematite can be placed on appliances to absorb the frequencies those machines put out. Be sure to cleanse the stones well when you're done. Generic negative energy: This is the classic consideration that normally fits into most ritual formulas. This energy collects from arguments in a space, negative thoughts generated there, or just from a lack of movement within the area. Generic negative energy can be broken up by a simple sweep with a besom. Herbs such as sage, basil, or black pepper can be burned on coals and taken through the space. Generic positive energy: The type off stuff you actually want to have floating around. So the opposite of the above. Astral temple: Building an astral temple is a powerful process that establishes your physical space in the Otherworld. This is something that is meant more for space that you want to establish as sacred permanently. It's great for a covenstead or a room in your home that is dedicated entirely to spiritual work. The process can be as simple as literally building up the bricks of a place in your mind as you meditate within the space. Decorate it however you wish and add powerful features that set it up as a mystical establishment. For more information about building astral temples, I recommend reading *The Inner Temple of Witchcraft* by Christopher Penczak.

Shifting consciousness

This is often cited as some of the classic requirements of magick in general, although there is sometimes a lack of importance on this as a step in ritual, especially within a group setting. Another term used to describe this process is "shifting awareness". There is a difference though. When we shift consciousness, we are changing the experience we are having right there in that moment. It is something that is within our sphere of influence that we have the ability to change at any time. Awareness is an original state of being that does not go away. We think it changes but the only thing that changes is what we will it up with. Consciousness arises within awareness. Awareness is the cup that is filled with different angles of consciousness.

Why is shifting consciousness such an important step? The process we might think of as all mental, is really the shifting of a whole range of things. When you shift consciousness, you are also shifting the state of your subtle energy bodies, sending signals to your soul that tell it to wake up, and opening the channels of all the centers of power within your bodies. It's an important step because it really does set the stage for what comes next.

Summon powers

This step is mostly the combination of calling quarts, elements, etc. and raising energy. I combine them because calling formative forces to aid your process really is a form of raising energy. After all, evoking guardians or guides doesn't mean that you send them an invite and then kick back while they make stuff happen. If you make it a practice of calling directional spirits, then really engage them! So often do we invite them in at the start and then forget about them until they end when we "dismiss them." This has always just felt rude to me. When you invite guests to your home to a dinner party, do you ignore them until they go away? I don't know about you but at my house we entertain them or give them something to do. They have a purpose for being there and it isn't just to occupy space.

Raising energy is usually considered the "heart" of the ritual, the most important part. But remember that in this ritual formula, all steps are equally important. Because of this, we don't have to stress out about any perceived fragility involved in raising energy. Because so much emphasis is placed on this step, people can get very nervous about it. Planning ritual can get really intense at this point because you might become consumed with the decision of what the most effective method would be. In my opinion, the method doesn't matter in the slightest. What does matter is the energy itself and how much you can raise towards what you need to do. Yes, size does matter in this case. Remember that there are a number of barriers that magick has to get past in order for it to fully manifest. Granted most of these are self-made but it makes them no less real. Putting power into your work gives you a greater chance of success. It is just that simple.

Direct and seal

This will usually be seen as falling under the raising of the energy process as the end point of that step. However, I see the sending and sealing of energy as an important step unto its own. It is not enough to raise a fabulous supply of energy and then just vomit it into the universe. We have to shape it with definition, shape its course, give it a road map, and lock it into place once it's gone. Imagine travelling to a single important destination across the country with just passion and intuition alone. You could succeed, but a number of things would stand in your way and slow you down before you get there.

Consider the athame, which is the tool we use to direct the energy of the circle in many Craft traditions. The blade is used because it represents the effective will. It is sharp and hard, representing the cunning and strength we need to reach our goals. It is thin, allowing us to move it through the air with speed and accuracy. The handle is heavy, allowing us to have a firm grip and an anchor point to start from. When you send out the energy that you raise in circle, you are the athame. If your purpose and will is not sharp, your magick must work harder to make a difference. If your handle is not firm, your magick will take longer to take root (if it does at all). Daily practice is what will keep you "sharp" on a day to day basis, but the way you direct your energy on its own is important to consider.

Sealing your work is also called binding but I don't like the sound of "binding" when talking about magick. Binding implies that you're restricting your work and not giving it the trust it needs to flourish. Sealing on the other hand implies that you're stamping it shut and giving it a secure send off. It implies elasticity and the ability to bend. It's like shutting the trunk of your car. Binding is like nailing the trunk shut. Sealing is like closing it until it needs to be opened again. When we seal out magick after it's sent, we ensure that nothing "leaks out" or is wasted on the way. I like to seal my work with a simple affirmation and the ring of a bell. I might say something like:

This work is done for my highest good and may it serve me well.
I seal it tight love and trust, as I sound this bell.

Engagement

This is really just something to consider, but I feel that it is so important that it should be its own full step. In your ritual planning, consider this fifth step in the four other steps above this.

Ritual should engage the heart, mind and will. To be fully effective, all of these things matter, not just one of them. And really, if all of these things are not fully engaged in ritual, what's the point of ritual? Being engaged means having consciousness about what you're doing combined with the intention of doing it. We can be conscious about not being fully active. For example, watching too much television is a numbing act that dulls the senses and puts you into a sort of stasis. You may be conscious of this, but you likely aren't putting forth an intention to do that. On the flip side, you may have the intention of entering a 10 kilometer race, but you aren't conscious of the factors involved and the training you'll need to do in order to get there. Being engaged means that consciousness and intention dance together. When these two things kiss, being fully engaged and alive is the experience that is birthed.

We make choices about how engaged we want to be at every moment. Let's face it; being awake in the world is something that takes effort. If it were easy, we'd have a lot more brilliant people walking around and doing great things with their days. The choice we make each moment lays out the pattern of activity for the next. This shows up in ritual when we are planning our outline and performing each of the above steps for effective deep ritual. One affects the other and there is no disconnection. If disconnection occurs, it bursts a big hole in the ritual and greater energy and work is needed to make up for that. If your first step is rushed, unfocused or scattered, it is likely that the following step will be the same. For example, calming and centering a big group of energetic people can be challenging, especially if they're not used to doing this on their own before ritual. It is well worth the effort though as it will be much harder to get those folks' anchors enough to raise, direct, and seal energy later on. Why is that? Magick, like all energy, favors momentum. If you build up good momentum at the start of ritual by being fully engaged, nothing stands in your way from working strong magick.

Engaging the five physical senses

Powerful ritual is the result of engaging all of the senses, not just the psychic senses. The physical senses are more important than we give them credit for. The taste, touch, smell, sound and sight of ritual are all factors that we can use to our advantage. When we awaken these senses, we awaken the mysteries of the body and the powers the body holds.

Taste is experienced primarily through the sharing of "cakes and ale", usually towards the end of ritual. The breaking of bread with community is nothing new in religious practice. Its importance is seen in the communion rite in Catholicism where these tiny cardboard-like crackers are eaten to represent the body of Christ. The wine they drink is the blood of Christ. Cakes and ale aren't always made of cake and alcoholic beverage. In my own coven we have people who are vegan (including myself), gluten-free, have allergies, or don't drink alcohol at all. The substance doesn't matter as much as the experience.

Any kitchen Witch will tell you that food is quite a powerful thing. The tastes of a warm pie can bring me right back to my aunt's kitchen on Thanksgiving Day. A cool class of lemonade is the best way for me to connect with Younger Self and the humid summers I spent as a kid in Buffalo. Good tastes can make us feel comfortable and bring out commonalities in people who can't seem to get past other silly differences. There's a reason why potlucks are so popular in the Pagan community.

Working with taste in ritual doesn't mean that you need to become a master chef overnight. Everyone can make something that tastes good, even if it's just "prepared" rather than made from scratch. Taking the risk of working on a new recipe is a fabulous way to honor the gods for a feast day or sabbat. What are their sacred foods? What are the foods that the ancient culture of that god eats on a day to day basis? You can also think of the type of taste and how it will affect your mind and spirit. In general these are the factors I associate the various tastes with:

Bitter - Dark Goddess, Underworld mysteries, shadow work, protection
Sweet - Light God, Upperworld mysteries, love and passion, raising energy
Savory - Ancestors, spirit allies, healing, grounding
Sour - Divination, insight, renewal, new beginnings
Salty - Goals, success, cleansing, removing obstacles

Taste is very personal thing and you probably have some different or additional associations with the above. Take the time to figure out the type of energy you feel when experiencing these different tastes. Once you do, you can craft specific foods around ritual that can really enhance your work.

Touch is probably the sense we pay the least attention to in ritual but one that has a deep effect on us, even if only on the subtle level. The feel of the cold athame when you take it up and experience it growing warm to your touch. The smoothness of tumbled stones you place in your mojo bag. The heat of the candle flames on your face as you sit at your altar for daily practice. These are things we all experience but often take for granted.

One of the reasons why herbalism is my favorite magickal medium is touch. This isn't a common association with plant magick as most think of taste or smell when they think of herbs. When I was first learning about herbal magick, the feel of the herbs sifting through my fingers and crunching in my mortar and pestle really gave me a sensational feeling. We don't touch the Earth enough. Everything is sterile and we carry hand sanitizer around everywhere in our germ phobic modern world. Touching raw materials like plants brings us back to our basic nature as human beings.

Incorporating touch in ritual is easy. Most of it is mindfulness and paying attention to what you're touching. When leading a guided meditation, I like to have participants hold something, especially if it's not the type of meditation where they need to "totally disconnect." On Samhain I like to lead a meditative journey surrounding the story of the descent of Inanna into the Underworld. In the story, Inanna gave up various vestments to the gate keepers to be granted admission in her descent. One of them was a fabulous lapis necklace. In my meditation, I like to drop a single lapis bead into the hands of the participants as we approach this point. I ask them to run their fingers over the bead and feel its texture and temperature. I ask them to notice how the stone is cool at first but easily warms to the touch.

Using touch in this way can also act as a physical anchor when doing deep spiritual work. Anchors act as a grounding tool to keep us connected to Earth when we do journey work, astral travel, or deep mind exploration. Anchors are helpful because they establish a sense of security, telling the etheric body that it's ok to do what you need it to do. The reason some people can have such a hard time learning how to do astral projection on-command is that they wish to have no anchor point. They want to be free to fly around but ignore the needs of the mental self, which may require some coaxing.

Smell is one of the most acknowledged senses in ritual, aside from sight. Everything from candles, incense, oils, and even flowers on the altar can contribute to this highly stimulated sense.

Incense is a scented tool of rituals that has been in use since Neolithic times and is one of the oldest tools of human spiritual practice throughout all of humanity. Incense was burned by the ancient Chinese, Egyptians, and followers of Hinduism (and still is today). Historically, the preference for what to burn was placed on locally available ingredients. In using my own native lands of North America as an example – pine, cedar, and sage were all common ingredients that were and still are burned as offerings and sacraments to the Old Ones.

Witches of both antiquity and modern times know how to make use of various plants, barks, and resins as incense for ritual and other religio-magickal practices. The scent of the smoke has both a psychological and energetic effect. The scent triggers a response in the brain that lets it know that something mystical is about to happen. Of course, this is always the goal when doing anything designed to engage in ritual consciousness, but there is something unique about the use of incense to do this. At times when I sit at my altar and can't seem to focus or center myself, sometimes all I need is a good blend of incense to put me in the mood for the work ahead.

Recipe - devotional ritual incense

This incense blend is my own personal favorite for use in ritual, daily devotions, or even regular meditation work. Its scent provides a nice energetic background to the work at hand while consisting of ingredients that are traditional to magickal work in many places. One of the best parts about this blend is how flexible it is. All you need are three substances out of any ingredient on this list.

Mix together equal parts of any three of the following ingredients Myrrh, Frankincense, Copal, Sage, Cedar, Dragon's Blood, Rosemary, Lavender, Rose. For the flowers and herbs in the list, you'll want to make sure they are fully dried before blending. With a mortar and pestle, grind together three of those ingredients (my personal favorites are frankincense, myrrh, and rosemary) well. It is best to avoid reducing the mixture to a powder as you'll find that powders burn too quickly when placed on the blocks of incense charcoal.

Hearing is one of the more noticeable senses, perhaps just above smell. The sounds of ritual vary from ecstatic drumming and shouting to simple, pure silence. Most people who have been to several public rituals have been to both. And I would hope that anyone in solitary practice for any extended amount of time would have experienced both on their own as well. You may even have a favorite type, feeling that a different noise level may not "work for you." Well, you may not be able to make it work for you, but you can certainly have it work with you.

The power of sounds has never been understated in the Pagan religious experience. There's a reason why drum circles are so commonly found at Pagan and Witch Festivals. Sound can put us into deep calming trance or awaken us into a place of trembling excitement. Playing with sounds is something that we have a great ability to do whether solitary or in a group. Have you ever been into a haunted house attraction at Halloween time? If you have then you know how the eerie sound effects can add so well to the creep factor. This isn't metaphor, I've used the same sound effects in Samhain rituals centered around connection with shadow self and the Dark Mother. I've also used catchy pop music to raise energy and awaken stagnant energy.

Ritual for life

Ritual never stops for the Witch. For us, it is something that remains a part of our lives for the rest of our lives. Whether simple or ecstatic, the rites we perform over time have a long term effect on our bodies, minds, and spirits. What began as a body of basic organic elements becomes a vessel for the powers of the entire universe to mix and mingle with. Through ritual, we can celebrate life in ways that give us meaning, beyond just the joy of the celebration itself. In this way, ritual becomes something we live for entirely, rather than something we just do at the height of the full moon.

Somewhere, right now, someone is lifting a cup to the name of the Old Gods. Someone is working a magickal rite to transform their lives. Engaging in ritual means we connect with the very stuff that connects all of humanity together.

Chapter 8

Spinning the Wheel

Spring passes and one remembers one's innocence. Summer passes and one remembers one's exuberance. Autumn passes and one remembers one's reverence. Winter passes and one remembers one's perseverance.
- Yoko Ono

The observation of seasonal festivals is a commonality that spans across many Witchcraft-based traditions. Great emphasis is placed on these in Wicca, where eight primary festival days are observed. And even though the eight are not always observed in other traditions, certain days still remain holy. What is it about special days on the calendar that call to the Witch for celebration? How does one decide which are essential and which can be put aside? Usually tradition-specific observances are mandated within the text of that tradition itself. Instead, I propose that we look to the value of each day and think about how we place ourselves within the scope of the year.

Seasonal changes were always regarded as extremely important to all ancient cultures that relied on planting and harvest times for the survival of their people. In many areas we see the belief in spirits that could cause blessings or blight on harvest crops, which could potentially destroy an entire area of people by starvation. When you look at the history of food production in the United States and Europe, we discover that we only recently moved to the system we have now around one to two hundred years ago at max. In other words, I don't have to grow and harvest my own wheat to get a loaf of bread. I walk over to the grocery store and buy it for $3.99 a loaf. The entire process takes twenty minutes of my time.

What happens to the spiritual life of the Pagan person who is not involved with the everyday concerns of planting and reaping throughout the entire year? Does this lack of involvement mean that we cannot take part in the natural cycles of nature? Absolutely not. We just change our approach. As I mentioned earlier, Witchcraft is all about adaptation. We adapt because we work with the spirits and the spirits adapt. The spirits do not always like the ways in which they have to adapt, but they do it to survive and to continue to play a part in their existence and the existence of what is around them. Witches today do not practice the same Witchcraft that might have been around five hundred years ago. No matter what any fifth generation grand poobah hereditary Witch tells you, no one knows exactly what Witches were doing more than a few generations ago. We can't look into documentation about the magick-workers of old in most places without finding history that is colored with accusatory language by witch-finders and the scribes of the inquisition. What we can do is look to our ancient past and make good guesses. We can take our findings and combine them with what we know works today. In terms of honoring earth festivals, the result of that is a syncretic tradition that is modern with some very ancient roots.

Think of the wheel of the year in Wicca for instance. On it we see eight holidays divided very neatly across the whole year. Four days for the solstices and equinoxes, and four days that fall in between. As much as we would like to say the wheel is a complete surviving system of holidays, it is not. The wheel is perhaps the most interesting amalgamation of traditions that exist within the craft today. It's a great example of the combining of traditions that make a perfectly blended system that's quite useful for crafters today. From the Teutonic peoples we get the solar festivals of the solstices and equinoxes (Yule, Ostara, Litha, and Mabon) and from the Celts we get the harvest celebrations (Imbolc, Beltane, Lughnassadh, and Samhain).

I love this arrangement personally because it represents some of the cultures of which I am a part. For those who don't have Celtic or Northern European ancestry, you can still appreciate the myriad of ways in which these cultures have contributed to and enriched the lore of the Craft (and much of neopaganism as a whole) throughout the ages. Celebrating these days aligns us with the spiritual heritages of people who went to great lengths to achieve spiritual communion with nature. By immersing ourselves in the sabbats of the wheels and other days, we can achieve the same.

This chapter will explore some of the notable holy days sacred to Witches and other modern natured-based magick-workers. Rather than dive too deeply on the intellectual history of these days (refer to the bibliography for a great number of books on that), we will instead focus on how to align ourselves with the powerful forces at work around the many days of power.

Samhain

In the original tradition I was trained in, Samhain is considered the "first" sabbat of the year on the wheel. Although some traditions will say Yule is really the first sabbat, neither claim would be totally true. After all, these days are continuously in process and our year is not linear, it is circular.

Samhain is the dying time, but there is much we can create. The days around October 31 bring a chilling and exciting feeling in the air. Part of this could be that I just love the middle of fall. I love the crunch of the leaves under my boots and the smell of the crisp autumn air. But I think there is more to it than that. We know that on Samhain, the veils that cloak the boundary lines between the worlds wane thin. Because of its close parallel to the modern secular celebration of Halloween, the images of ghosts and spirits are closely linked to this time of year. This would be an accurate assessment, as many people believe it to be the one time of the year that the dead have "free reign" to skip over into our worlds. It is also for this reason that Samhain time is one of the most feared and respected holy days as well.

Samhain corresponds to the planet Pluto and the zodiacal sign of Scorpio. Pluto is the planet of the dead and corresponds to the Greek god of the dead, Hades. Like Halloween, Hades is feared and respected by the Hellenic people who nowadays even shy away from saying his name directly.

Working with death

Just like the Halloween season, the powers of death are uniquely linked to the Witch all throughout history. While we don't know precisely what the exact function of the Witch was in ancient times, we do know that one of her main personas was that of the necromancer. Necromancy has quite a nefarious image in the Craft today. It can undoubtedly be a dangerous thing if one does not know what they're doing, but as with any system that works with the energies of the Otherworld, there will always be a certain risk.

Working with the dead is something I consider to be absolutely essential to every form of Witchcraft there is. No matter how you cut it, we are a people that live off the legacy and power of our ancestors and others who came before us. This is not metaphor; it is a very literal association that cannot be unhinged from the magickal arts. For many years in the beginning of my practice I struggled with the amount of time I needed in order to engage with this energy. To be honest, the way I was trained did not highlight working with death in any important way, other than on Samhain night itself. I thought ancestor worship was just something a few people did, but wasn't for me. That was until I actually started doing it with some consistency.

Samhain is the perfect time to begin to work with the dead if you have not begun to already. If you already do this work, then consider it a great time to recommit to this practice and strengthen your relationships with the beloved dead. In the dying time of October and November, the dead are much more likely to pay attention to you. That attention brings a wonderful opportunity to make a connection that can last a lifetime.

Why is it so important to work with the dead? The answer to this will likely vary depending on which Witch you ask. For me, it is my shamanic view of the Craft that colors my outlook on the world of the human discarnate spirits. If part of my job is to act as an intermediary between the worlds, then having a healthy team of allies in this work is essential. When I am travelling between the veils, there is a risk I take each time, however small it may be. Having a strong relationship with the dead means I can traverse these worlds with more confidence and meaning than if I did not. It is also practical for the sake of our magick. The dead – though existing beyond the immediate reaches of this world – are still intimately connected to it. They lived here before. They had their manifest being on this plane of existence. As so, they are likely to take an interest in what happens to us here. And if they are allies, their interest lies within the desire to see you succeed in all your ventures.

Altar of the dead and spirit devotionals

I do know many Witches who maintain at least a basic ancestral altar. What trips me up is the assumption by some that these can only hold space for blood ancestors. This is why I prefer to call it an altar of the dead in general, rather than an ancestor altar. Although one could argue that all beings who come before us are ancestors in the grand scheme of things, it feels limiting to think of this space as existing only for the beloved dead of one's physical family. Having an altar for spirits of the dead we know in addition to the "spirit of death" in general can be a powerful way to connect into the current of the dying time, at all times of the year.

If you already maintain an ancestor altar, try expanding it to the spirits of others you admire, however old. I even have a couple of photos of some American Revolutionary War heroes on mine. If you don't have any such altar, Samhain is the perfect time to create and dedicate one. The key to diving deeper here is to use it in ways that enrich your spiritual life rather than just setting one up as a decoration and not paying it beyond a passing glance. Some things to keep in mind when creating or recreating the altar of the dead might be:

Spending time before its creation collecting a vast array of meaningful images and items to represent the dead. These can be photos, trinkets, letters, or even printed papers with information about the person.

Obtain something to represent the spirit of death itself. On my own altar, I have a simple white porcelain skull. The back of it has a cupped space the perfect size for a small tea candle. When I call upon the spirit of death in whatever form, I can rub this image and light the candle inside it. Be creative here.

Research the favorite food and drinks of the dead on your altar. You will then have the information you need to make highly effective offerings to the person on their birth or death dates (or just on Samhain itself). If you can't obtain this information, gifts of barley, wine, apples, and bread are all traditional offerings to the dead.

Leave safe spots for candles to burn on the surface so you can light them periodically whenever you desire. Then, get the candles. My favorite candles to keep on these altars are the large seven-day glass jar candles (also called "Saint Candles"). Some say white is the perfect color for candles of the dead because it represents the purity of the afterlife. For magickal reasons, I prefer black as I work with the dead in ritual as well. The color black acts as a magnet, drawing in helpful spirits for your work. A fun pre-Samhain craft would be attaching images and charms to one of these candles in honor of a specific person. I think the dead really appreciate things like this that give their image a special "glow" (literally) on this plane.

Exercise – Declaring the altar and giving offering

Once your altar of the dead is up to par, you'll want to formally recognize it as a nexus point of power and reverence. We'll do this a few ways and several of the steps can be repeated at any point. Again, the time around Samhain would be an excellent time to perform this work. We will first open the veils and speak the names of the dead. Then, we will sanctify the space and close with offerings. To prepare for the rite, you might mix up an incense appealing to the dead. If you'd like to make your own, here's a sample recipe which is the one I use.

Spirit Offering Incense
1 part mugwort
1 part wormwood
1 part lavender
1 part rosemary
½ part mullein leaf
1 pinch of graveyard dirt from a loved one's grave

I find this mixture works well to not only get the attention of the dead, but also to open up my psychic senses. This way, I can feel out the process of the work and measure its success by way of intuition. Obviously to generate smoke you'll need to burn on an incense charcoal. However, you can also gift small piles of this as a whole on its own in a small dish. Smoke is preferred as it has a greater ability to traverse the worlds, but the solid stuff is acceptable.

When ready, stand before the altar and enter a light trance state. Feel your awareness fall inwards as you focus on the blood. Feel it pumping through your body and sense its power. This awareness will conjure up the essence of your Witch Blood that connects you with all who have gone before. Continue the trance work for a few more moments until you lift your awareness back into your head. At this point, you can begin to visualize and sense the images of the beloved dead whom you're dedicating the altar too. Take time for each one you know who will take a permanent (or semi-permanent) place upon the altar.

We will now begin to speak the names of the dead. Take up your wand and tap the surface of the altar three times and then trace an invoking pentagram in the air before you. Speak out the words:

> I call to the hallowed void! The space from which the Star Goddess looked upon herself in holy reflection. Birther of all time, from which the endless procession of wanderers sprang forth.
>
> Be present in this space and open the way for communion with the beloved dead. Let not those of ill will or malicious intent cross the veil into this holy place. Instead, open the way for those invited and welcomed guests: [say the full names of the dead here...]

At this point you may lay the offerings on the altar. If you have prepared an incense offering, pour some on the coals or place the dish of solid mixture on the surface. If you would like to pour them some wine or present food, you can do this now as well. When the offerings are presented, speak the words:

> As the priests of old have always done, I approach this temple of the dead with solemn reverence and the gifts of my memory. For all who are remembered live. The gifts of the solid earth breathe the joys of a life once lived into the place where my beloved rests. And thus I place the holy offerings upon this place, so made for the dearly departed – that they may know of the honor I give them.

Stand in silent reflection for whatever amount of time you like. If you desire to light candles, you can do so now. From here out, you should feel free to approach the altar of the dead at any time to light the candles or lay offerings. I try to make time to do this a few times per week. Around Samhain time, I do it every day.

When your time of reflection has ended, take up the wand and trace a banishing pentacle in the air before you. Tap the surface of the altar three times again. It is done.

Attuning to the death mysteries

Death is a mystery and as such can never be understood fully unless you – well – die. If learning of the death mysteries is such an important part of the Craft, how can we expect to explore it fully? How can we begin to understand mentally and spiritually this vital topic? Like anything in the Craft, we learn by feeling and doing. No, I don't want you to physically die right now. Our theology is important in that most of us believe that in some way, we have died before. Whether you believe that death occurred in another physical human life or it occurred within the first blasts of the big bang, we take a strange comfort in knowing that our "immortal" souls have experienced endings before.

In Wicca, we find the idea that death brings a journey to a place of rest called the Summerland. In this place of immense beauty and joy, we take a pause and review the life we lived. We look at our accomplishments and our failures. We take stock of who we have helped and who we harmed. There is no judgment here, just a deep understanding of the bigger picture we all painted within.

Whether you hold belief in the Summerland or some other type of post-life resting place is irrelevant for our purposes here. When we explore Witchcraft to its depths, we instead place focus on the journey of things rather than the destination. The journey of death is one of those core ideas that most religious and spiritual systems on this planet share. We don't just sit there in our bodies, we move on, go somewhere, or turn into something else. Again I am reminded of the correlations between the Witch and the shaman who both traverse the worlds for a greater understanding of the mysteries.

When we look at the Death card in many traditional tarot systems, we find death as a skeletal being atop a horse, scythe in hand. Most people immediately look to the foreboding image of the scythe, the tool of the reaper. However, I tend to look at the horse. The horse is a prominent image, not an afterthought, suggesting larger importance be placed upon *where* death is going rather than who it's going *for*. It is also often white in color, pointing to the symbolism of new beginnings, the culmination of many things, and the power of refreshing possibility. When the death card shows up in a reading, it is often interpreted as a wonderful possibility for new things to come in. It is the ability to access new power by realizing that you can destroy the obstacles that stand in the way of success. Like the knightly skeleton in the death card, we can charge forward with certainty and a sense of mission. Those tarot artists can be pretty deep, eh?

The runic equivalent of the death card is often thought to be Thurz. Thurz is the rune of thorns and like the death card, is many-faceted and frequently misunderstood. When Thurz shows up in my rune readings, it often points to the need for will to rise up and join the pathways of desire for the person to get to the place they need to be. As we discussed in our section about will in the fire chapter, will is essential spiritual growth and the performance of all successful magick. Without will, we are nothing. Without will, we would not have the ability to live or die. The beings of the angelic realms do not live or die and it is our will that exists in the mortal realms that they lack. It is for this reason that these beings consider us more privileged than they are. Thurz reminds us that part of being human is wading through the thorns, bleeding, and coming out better for it by way of our experience, our ability to feel something. For another symbol of the death mysteries, we look to the image of the pomegranate. One of the most beloved and revered death images, it is the fruit that tempted Persephone to stay with Hades in the Underworld for a number of months within the year. The pomegranate shows us that just as the middle and upper worlds contain things both sweet and lovely, so too can the lower worlds. The bittersweet taste of endings and reprieve tell us that there is still value and power and living after you have lived here within the mortal coil.

Exercise – Attune with the death mysteries

Gather the images discussed above; a death card from the tarot, an image of Thurz, a pomegranate or other such symbols that connect humanity to the mysteries of death. If you can find whole parts of the plants used in the spirit offering incense, that would be excellent. Most people will have access to bundles of fresh rosemary at the local supermarket year-round. Decorations such as skulls, dark stones, and shroud fabric would also be appropriate for this rite.

Arrange the items around you in a circle with a diameter the length of your body from head to toes. Place one black candle in the northern part of the circle, close enough to the edge where you can move around a bit. You'll be sitting on your bottom and scooting around for this.

To start the rite, take some sort of protective measures of whatever form you like. We are opening to energy that is of the deepest type to the realm of humans. What we will gain is a long-term understanding of the power of death and a stronger relationship with the spirits. This work is not dangerous but the influx of energy from this other world could feel jarring. Imagining a ring of blue fire around the circle will be enough to stabilize the energy you're calling in to attune with.

Begin by lighting the candle and staring at the flame. Breathe slowly and relax deeply. Feel the edges of your skin become fuzzy as you expand your etheric body, mingling with the energies of the otherworld surrounding you. Focus on the blue part of the candle flame as you allow the space around you to fall away. The outside of the circle deepens in tone until it turns black.

Take up the first symbol that's directly in front of you. Stare at it in the same way you did the candle flame. With your intuition guiding you, say a line or two to attune with that symbol. For example, you might say something like: "oh pomegranate, sweet seduction of our Queen Persephone, attune me to your powers." Continue in this way moving around the circle clockwise taking up each symbol until you reach the north again.

Repeat the process of staring at the flame but only for a moment. Feel the outside world returning into focus. At this point you could likely feel any number of things ranging from extreme physical energy to an influx of low-vibration energy (causing a feeling of being "drained"). Sit with whatever feeling you get and take a mental note of it. It will be useful to call upon this feeling in the future while doing things like approaching the altar of the dead. Extinguish the candle and it is done.

Assisting the dead and those who remain

The Witchcraft I practice is very service-oriented and the death of someone does not remove me from that duty. Some other Witches feel the same which is why a few of us feel called to also practice mediumship, attend (or lead) funeral rites, and on occasion perform exorcism. Making ourselves available for difficult tasks like these can be some of the most rewarding actions that public Craft provides. We are acting as intermediaries between the beings of this world and the next, making ourselves a true visible nexus point of power. It is clear to see that this work also flows over into our personal magick, especially around Samhain and the dying time.

I believe all Witches should at least familiarize themselves with one form of mediumship or spirit contact work. Not only for the practical reasons of being able to commune with the dead to a greater capacity, but also because it expands our vibration in a way that allows for a wider channel of intuitive energy to flow in. The Witch who is also a medium can provide hope and healing for community members who lose a loved one and need to move on as part of the grieving process. For many people, having a sense of validation that the person's spirit is doing something outside the bonds of the flesh can be incredibly healing.

The Witch as minister is a subject that lives far beyond the scope of this book, but I will discuss it briefly here in terms of one of the most important rites these people are called to perform. Even if you do not choose to walk the path of ministry, you will likely be called upon at some point to at least lead an observance for someone who has crossed over. In our spiritually-jaded world, you will be a light to people around you in times of grief and will be looked to for facilitation of funerary rites like this. Learn all you can about them. Do spirit contact work with the being ahead of time and ask them what would be the most helpful and healing for their loved ones who still live. You can see the great advantage that Witches have when doing work like this. As we serve both the living and the dead, we should look to methods that assist both when approaching these tasks.

Occasionally, you might come across a spirit that exists by nefarious means. Again, the spirit contact work is so valuable here because most of what we think of as a "violent haunting" can be chalked up to a classic case of past event manifestation, or at worst, poltergeist activity. In most cases performing a rite that encourages the spirit to move on is all that is necessary. However, some discarnate beings know they should not be in the place they are and take power by frightening or harming the living. In these cases, an exorcism is necessary. Exorcism can be performed on a home, a land space, an object, and yes – even a person.

Exercise – A simple rite of exorcism

For anyone who has seen the movie "The Exorcist", seeing an actual rite of exorcism from the magickal traditions might seem shockingly simple, and often times they are. I like to think that's because Witchcraft – being a Craft that naturally works with the spirits – can pack more of a punch when dealing with nefarious spirits than those who do not work with spirits in a positive way at all. This sample rite is designed for exorcism of the home but could easily be adapted for other scenarios.

Get a large container of salt which we will use to cover much of the house. If you have a large home, you may want to get a couple of containers. Any salt is fine but I like to use sea salt for its added water properties (water being the element of cleansing power). For ease of use in the rite, I like to pour all the salt into a consecrated bowl for easy empowerment at my altar. Again, this is preference.

Have the salt before you and take up the wand. In broad gestures, wave the wand all around in a clockwise motion and imagine all the positive energies of the home being gathered up in the air around you and collecting in a sphere of blinding light at the tip of the wand. Speak these words:

By the power of my sacred domain, I bless you O creature of earth
Be for me a tool of warfare and might, of sovereign love and unwavering strength.
By the power of the holy land spirits and the spirits of my blood and kin,
let the power to purify and cast out be known within every single grain of this salt.
So mote it be!

On the "so mote it be" part, swing the wand down pointing towards the salt and pour all the gathered light into it. Imagine every grain of salt transforming into a tiny little sphere of light.

Take the salt around the home and lay piles of it in strips across every doorway and window threshold. If you have hardwood floors (or carpet with a very good vacuum), scatter it all around the ground as well. Scatter it on countertops and tables, in the sinks and on the toilet lids. Pour it everywhere you think you'll be able to while still having the ability to easily clean it up later. When this is done, stand in the center of the house and say:

I cast you out, O unclean thing
By the salt of the earth and the spirits of my blood and kin
Depart from this place and let the gods do with you what they will,
*   as long as it is away from me and mine.*
Within three miles of every grain of salt scattered here, you cannot
*   be.*
I revoke your residence and cast you out. I cast you out. I cast you
*   out!*

You can now either clean up the salt immediately or let it sit for a little while overnight. When you clean it up, get as much of it up as possible. The method of disposal does not matter. If you performed this around Samhain time, the time after would be well used by communing with the spirits of good intentions in your life. Spend some time calling those spirits back to you or giving them honor. Truth be told, using salt in ritual has a tendency to push away *all* spirits, even if that was not the intent. With this rite you specifically mentioned that only unclean beings be pushed away, so don't fret so much over that aspect.

Samhain as gateway

The veils being thin at this time of year doesn't mean that only spirits can shift easily between the worlds – we can too! In the time of death, take opportunities each day to commune with the idea that all passings are an opportunity for something to begin anew. What are those little deaths in life that end up bringing you greater purpose and meaning? The energy of this time can be used to skyrocket you into a place of greater connection with all the things you wish to begin.

To utilize this at full capacity, come up with little ways you can reflect on the process of moving from one place to another. In observing the wheel, I feel that folks too often only focus on Samhain as "ending" and Yule as "beginning." But what fills that silent space between? Where do the ideas of rest and the reclaiming of power fit into your life at this time? In Qabalah, this time could be related to "Daath", the invisible sphere that represents the void on the way to Kether, the formless divine. Ask yourself, "What is my process at this time? What am I becoming?"

November – The time of void

The whole month of November is what I consider to be Daath, that invisible sphere mentioned above. It is often ignored as being simply a transition point from one sabbat to another. It certainly is a transition, but there is nothing simple about it.

Although I refer to November as "The Time of Void" here, I want to point out that because something is a void, does not mean that nothing exists within it. It has even been determined that black holes in space aren't just spaces of "nothing." There is something going on there, beyond what we are ever likely to see. In certain Craft traditions such as Anderson Feri and Wildwood, it is believed that God Herself looked upon herself in the mirror of the void and fell in love. In the process of reflection, she initiated the process of becoming. We can do this too.

November mirror magick

Using the idea of November as the void, spend this month working all forms of mirror magick. Most mirror magick in the beginning of Craft training is focused on the mirror as a tool for divination. While it is certainly a powerful tool for this work, there is so much more it can do. We can use the mirror just as Goddess does, to look upon ourselves and realize the miracle that is our existence. In particular, here are a few ideas for things you can do with a mirror in the void time (or really any time):

Have a "staring contest" with yourself. Gaze in your mirror and look deep into the pools of your eyes. Let your focus relax and allow the staring to trigger a trance state. The eyes are windows to the soul. What does your soul tell you when you stare right at it? Use your mirror to practice shapeshifting. Shapeshifting is a powerful and ancient practice used to aspect a variety of natural powers. Usually these powers are animal in nature. After beginning the practice above, feel your face begin to ripple and transform as you call up a power animal. As the ripples in the skin continue, see them changing color and texture until you find yourself transformed into the image of the animal. Speak to it. What is it telling you? All animals have a special medicine to share with humanity. Use a large mirror as a doorway into other worlds. If possible, bring a large body mirror into your circle and design a ritual meant to consecrate it as a doorway to wherever you desire to go. In a trance state, you can astral step into the mirror. Just like Alice walking into Wonderland, you can experience some strange and fascinating things here. Keep your intention clear and have a strong purpose for doing this. I also suggest bringing a guide along.

Throughout November, look to other things that serve the same function as a mirror in the metaphorical sense. What are the tools at your disposal that provide you with feedback? If you read the beginning of this book, your first answer should be journaling. Other tools such as pendulums and other divinatory tools can be used to help you recognize your process in the time of the void.

Yule – The birth of light

Winter Solstice, or Yule, can be thought of as a "destination" after we finish crossing the void time after Samhain. At this point, you will have done a lot of serious reflective work and are likely excited to focus outwards again. However, it is good to remember that Yule is a time of great darkness as well, although in a different form than Samhain was. After all, the Winter Solstice takes place on the shortest day of the year and the longest night. We can think of Yule as the process of birth itself, rather than the product of it. At this point in the year, the light is starting to return but has not yet fully manifested. The Once and Future King, the sun god, is being born.

At this time of the year, my family loves to light candles and potpourri. The week of Christmas, my mother always has festive candles burning away and scented oils warming on the stove. The senses really come alive when you walk into that house. Stepping off the plane from where I live in Washington DC and entering her house in North Carolina, I immediately feel the warmth of welcoming and togetherness. This is why this time of year is so captivating. For many ancient European and North American peoples, farming was impossible in the month of December and it was unnecessary to step outside. People got bored and irritated and invented customs and traditions to "keep the light alive" until they could go back out.

In the time of the birth of light, we look to the things we wish to begin in our lives and in our Craft. This is why that reflective work of the previous months was so important. We can now set goals and make promises for our work ahead. We can ask ourselves "what is my wish for this year?" Though in many places the icy winds are only beginning to blast, we can take advantage of the profound sense of hope and joy covering the planet by celebrants of many religious traditions.

Exercise – Attuning to joy

The joy that winter holidays bring to people all over the world is so strong it is nearly tangible. Whether you call it Christmas spirit, Yuletide joy, or holiday cheer, this feeling has its own egregore. It has lived and moved throughout so many generations and is so deeply embedded into our cultures that it has taken on a power all its own. It is so strong that it can be almost overwhelming at times. This is where the dreaded holiday burnout comes from and could also be the reason why many people become depressed after the December holidays.

The wise Witch can use the energy of this joyful egregore and ride its wave well into the spring. If practiced at the right time and with the right attitude, capturing joy and attuning with it can be a delightful experience and quite empowering for the practitioner. It's simple too.

Obtain a large pillar candle sometime in the first half of December, or whenever holiday activities start to really heat up where you live. This can vary by area. Inscribe the image of the sun and any accompanying symbols you desire (the joy rune Wunjo would be a nice addition) onto the candle. Anoint the candle with any solar or wintery oils such as frankincense, spearmint, cinnamon, orange, bay, clove, or high john.

Take the dressed candle outside or to a window at sunrise. Preferably, you would let the rays of the morning sun fall upon the candle as you simultaneously feel those rays heating the surface of your skin. Tune your mind to the power of joy adrift on the air of your local area. Say a silent prayer to the spirits of the land of your area asking them to connect you with this power. Ask for this power to become permanently linked to the candle, now and forever. When you feel sufficiently connected to the spirit of joy, light the candle and keep it lit for part of your morning. You can then light it every morning to give you a boost of joy in the day, or whenever you could use a dash of happiness. The candle can also be lit with the intention of sending joy to people in other areas who need it. I have found this works particularly well for people who suffer from seasonal mood disorder. You could even make a few small versions of these candles and pass them out as magickal gifts for the holidays.

Joy comes in many forms for the Witch. The greatest channels of joy can be found in finding partnership with the beings and intelligences of nature. Nature is a cunning vixen too. She is both lovely and cruel, sensible and erratic, all at the same time. She teaches us that outside of the wild swings of extreme sorrow and extreme ecstasy, there is a simple joy. The joy of being present in the slowly turning tides of the Earth and whatever that turning brings.

What solar tides teach

As the light increases from Yule onwards, we really begin to feel the solar tides come in. The solar tides make themselves visibly known whenever you can actually notice the shortening or elongating of the days. This can vary for each person depending on the area and the person's awareness of the seasons, but typically in North America and the UK, most really take notice of the tides once the winter solstice passes. Personally, I take great joy when I notice that the day is just starting to lengthen. For me this is usually around one week after winter solstice. In late December, it's usually pitch black outside by the time I leave work, so I very much relish in the strengthening sun.

The solar tides remind me of the concept of the Child of Promise mythos that often accompanies this time of year. The tiny arms of the child of the Earth are gently reaching towards the sustenance of the sun. As the result, the Earth Mother tilts her body to satiate her child with the rays of the sun he so craves. We are all reaching for the light in some way. Our humanity craves it because without it, we could not have our existence in any way.

This primal desire for the new light can fuel our magick in beautiful ways. When we step into the tides of the sun, we connect with the very essence of life itself. It is for this reason that so many systems of both classical and folk magick all consider the sun a symbol of success and power. It is the outward expression of our recurring victory over the forces of death. It tells us (and our magick) "after the greatest darkness, will come the new dawn." When attuning to the awareness of the tides (which is as simple as noticing the increasing hours of daylight each week), you plug in to that sense of victory and success. Attach your magick to that feeling and see the speed at which it manifests.

Exploring the mysteries of birth

Everyone reading this has either given birth, been born from someone, or both. If you count the possibility of past lives into the mix, then everyone has experienced both countless times. The mythos of the Child of Promise is centered around the mysteries of birth. Yule is an interesting time because we immediately make a switch from the powers of death and dying and look towards birth. I used to think this very strange as nothing new seems to grow in December where I live. If anything, it often gets colder after the winter solstice all the way up until March. Even so, there is a gentle awakening that the winter solstice brings.

The mysteries of birth are just as deep as those of death. I know some Witches chose to place more emphasis on the death mysteries, saying that because it is more of a mystery in the physical sense, then surely that must be the case in the spiritual sense as well. I must disagree here. We cannot *see* birth in the sense of the soul entering the body any more than we can see death once the soul leaves it. They are mysteries because even though we can speculate the theology and attempt to break it down with science, we cannot know the full capacity of what these things mean until we experience them for ourselves.

Luckily for us, we can approach the mysteries of birth just as we can with those of death. Exploring this means we access a deep well of power located within the root chakra, the area of our sex and survival. For our purposes here, we will do this via a guided mediation in trance.

Exercise – Meditation on birth

You might find it helpful to have someone read you this meditation or even record your own voice and play it back. I have done the latter and there is something strange and powerful about hearing your own voice for trance induction. However strange it feels at first, it does work. Otherwise, you'll need a dark and quiet place where you cannot be disturbed so you can focus on your own internal thoughts which will guide the meditation.

Relax and begin to breathe deeply. Relax every single muscle of your body from the top of your head down to your toes. Use the trance induction breaths we learned early on in the book or a system of your own choosing. Whatever works for you can be incorporated for this. Keep your eyes closed and if possible, blindfolded to ensure that no light gets past your eyelids. Once you feel sufficiently relaxed, lay on the floor on your back with your knees bent, legs arched.

In your mind's eye, feel yourself floating in the dark void of space. The space that was before God birthed Herself into existence. This space has no temperature or shape. No sound or texture. There is only the vast nothingness of time before time came along with your own thoughts. You float along gently, allowing any thoughts that pop up to pass by and disappear, leaving you to focus only on the black. After you have achieved a certain sense of oneness with this space, start to feel the edges of your skin tingle a little bit. Slowly feel tiny particles from all across the void start to flow to where you feel your central core is. The particles begin to move and as they do, you notice that there is a gentle light around them. And as they gather more heavily upon you, you begin to notice that you yourself are glowing slightly. You are like a star being formed after a period of great destruction. You realize now that you are an impossible existence that is coming into manifestation anyway. Breathe in this wondrous feeling as the particles continue to flow towards you and make up the form of your physical body. The complex strands of DNA that comprise our animal bodies are beginning to organize themselves within you now.

As the light continues to build within and around you, you find that you are becoming a tangible being floating in the vast darkness. In your mind you look down and notice your feet. You rejoice internally at the excitement of having a body. Slowly the other parts of you begin to form themselves out of the luminescent light. Eventually you discover the light has success-fully built you up into a fully tangible human being. You place your hand to your chest and feel the gentle pumping of your newly-formed heart. You listen closely as you hear the swish and swirl of your blood traveling through the narrow channels of your veins. Feel what it means to be human and all the potential that brings for your future. Eventually, the harsh blackness of the void begins to soften and allows some other subtle colors to come in. Shades of magenta and indigo lighten up the space around you. Something is stirring around you and you become aware of the heartbeat of another. The space around you starts to turn and push you from side to side. Your heart beats faster with excitement and anticipation. It feels like a new experience yet strangely familiar all at the same time. The force becomes more tumultuous as you feel yourself falling out of the dark void towards a single point of light in the distance. The light becomes larger as you continue to fall towards it. Eventually, the light becomes larger than the darkness around you which departs as you find that you're in a new world.

Notice what your body and souls feel like in this new world. Contemplate the mysteries of birth both literal and figurative. Every new idea you have or action you take is the conception of something. What do you desire to bring all the way into full manifestation? What do you choose to leave behind in the void? These are the things the winter solstice and the Yuletide mysteries of birth teach us.

January – Animal nature

January brings the bitter cold dampness of winter and no huge holidays (unless you count New Year's Day, which some do). I often think of January as a reflection of November but on the other side of the spectrum of things. While November is the journey of the void before birth, January is the journey towards growth after the initial birth of the light. It is the time when the lower-self, our animal nature, begins to grow and reach for the things it desires.

Of all animals, the wolf takes center stage in January, giving the name of the January full moon the "Wolf Moon." The wolf was greatly feared and respected by many European peoples in January as the deep winter brought the same risk of starvation for them as it did the humans. They become more desperate for food at this time and people would be (and still are in many places) cautious of an encounter with one. The wolf then becomes a symbol for the primal need for survival within the depths of the still-darkened season. The cry of the howling wolf becomes a spell to awaken our animal nature, which awakens the realization of what our primal urges are. This is deep knowledge that gives the ability to inform so many other parts of ourselves.

My own coven takes advantage of the Wolf Moon in a ritual to call upon the spirit of this mysterious animal. We call upon wolf to not only bring us its unique medicine, but also to wake up the animal self. For the solitary Witch, you can call upon the animal self by breathing deep into all the lower parts of the body. The animal self responds to simple language and can be asked very direct questions. Some questions for animal self that provide useful information for the Witch would be:

What is my most primal desire right now?
What is my most immediate need?

What is the state of my relationship with my tribe(s)?

Where do I need to draw power from to see me through the dark time?

Journal on these questions and ponder them throughout the month. You could even create entire rituals seeking some answers for them.

Imbolc and February

For our next Celtic-based festival we find what I believe to be one of the most underscored sabbat days. The history and tradition around Imbolc is both interesting and highly engaging for the Witch looking to do deep work. This day is another liminal time, starting at sundown on February 1st and lasting until sunrise on February 2nd. It's at this point in the year when many people start experiencing cabin fever and become frustrated with the persistence of the cold. Even though the light is increasing in dramatic amounts, it is a small consolation compared with the icy winds that still blast. I don't generally enjoy the cold so this is the point in the year when I'm just plain sick of putting layers on. Thousands of years of civilization have gone by yet we are still subject to things like cabin fever. Isn't nature interesting? Imbolc celebrates Brigit, a being considered both goddess to the Pagans and saint to the Catholics. She is a goddess who retained so much of her lore and imagery after the Christian conversion that she really deserves a day all for her own. It is likely that the earlier Crafters of Wicca agreed with this which is why Imbolc won a spot amongst the other seven sabbats on the wheel of the year. She is many things. A goddess who fills a multitude of positions such as smithcrafter, healer, fire-keeper, teacher, warrior, and poet. Brigit is powerful because all of these roles she fills are tied together and are not merely "aspects" of compart-mentalized tasks she performs. All of her skills flow together in a way that makes her a truly unique goddess for this newly emerging age.

One of Brigit's most famous roles, that of the smith, is among the most important of all archetypes in Witchcraft. As we discussed earlier in the book in our mention of alchemy, this idea of welding and melting different things together to create something new and beautiful speaks to our higher self in ways that are of great benefit to the Witch. As a form of art, we bring all of our disparate parts and parts of nature together to create something new and beautiful.

When we engage and create, Imbolc reminds us that within the depths of the darkness comes the bright shining light. Imbolc was also called Candlemas as it was the day when the Catholic priests would bless all the candles for the year at once. The focus on tools of light has its own obvious Pagan origins and it is something we still practice today. It is traditional on Imbolc to make and light candles in honor of the strengthening sun. The practice of lighting blessed candles is nothing new to even the most basic Crafter, but Imbolc brings an opportunity to explore the ways in which the solitary lights of the candle flame can enrich our spirits and bring inspiration to our minds. If Yule is about the search for light and the birthing of it into the world, then we might say that Imbolc is about taking that light and giving it a useful container for our work.

Exercise – Create a soul candle

Most of us have made or personalized candles in some way for spellcraft and magick. Candle magick is popular because it works. Here we have this little tool comprised of all the elements coming together to hold a continuously burning flame. Candles are soothing to the spirit human because of their gentle glow and the reminder that while fire can be destructive, it can also be quite beautiful too. Candle magick allows us to work with the elements in a way that is both engaging and creative. The 101 candle magick (lighting a green candle for money, red for love, etc.) is wonderful, but there is so much more we can do with it.

If we let them, candles can tell the story of our soul and provide us with the ability to change that narrative to whatever we desire. This is the function of a soul candle.

The concept of the soul candle was an idea born out of my work with the solar tides. You can think of it as "phase II" of that work. Whereas with the tides we brought energy of the sun in, we are now taking that internal light and bringing it outwards to manifest our highest work. Working with the soul candle regularly can result in a feeling of becoming more self-possessed and awake in the world. It is also something you can burn while performing any type of soul alignment.

The soul candle's creation is quite simple and is a wonderful thing to do for Imbolc. Simply obtain a large pillar candle of your favorite color and scent. Some might like to get fancy and work with colors and scents in alignment with their astrological chart. Once you have the candle, inscribe things on it that describe not only your personality, but your passions, dreams, core characteristics, and anything you can think of that makes you tick. You can do this in words or symbols. The candle can then be burned to bring your inner self (animal self) into conversation with your outward expression (talking self). And that's all there is to it!

Imbolc's promise

February is still bitterly cold in most places, yet signs of the emerging spring are starting to pop up all over the place. Even the evergreens which seemed to never take a rest are renewing their greenery. In my own area, the arrival of Maryland's beloved daffodils is a true sign that Earth is beginning to warm up again.

Imbolc is nature's way of showing us trust. It's a wild promise that "this too shall pass", that the heavy snows will give way to the lush and fertile green. I am reminded of the ritual phrase "in perfect love and perfect trust." This is a helpful saying that speaks to several things. First, perfection in this sense does not necessarily mean flawless or infallible. Instead it means to say that the love and trust will come from the place of my highest good in accordance with what my spirit needs for that relationship to flourish. The perfection of love is that it is not infallible. That it's perfect because it was designed to sometimes (or frequently) be rough.

Imbolc's promise is not precise. It is wild and exists at the core of its mystery. It tells us to look at the promises and contracts we have made with ourselves and others. Are they still applicable or serving you well? Are they of benefit, or does it only entangle and restrict? Imbolc is all about breaking free from that which binds us so we can begin again anew. Evaluating these pacts we make with ourselves can be helpful in determining the nature of our present state and what we need to move forward. It is zooming in to the nitty gritty details of our complexes so we can then zoom out and see the bigger picture. The day before Imbolc begins, bring out your journal and start an entry entitled "my contracts." Throughout the next twenty-four hours add things to this entry that describe the various agreements you have made that still hold. These agreements can be those you made to yourself, to others, and to the gods. Be fearless here. Don't be afraid to write down those negative internal agreements. Those will be some of the most helpful ones to point out. For example; a negative agreement that I had with myself last year was "I will fill holes. Whenever I see something not being done, I will do it myself." Although well intentioned, this promise put me on the fast track to burnout and I was only able to avoid that by recognizing this little internal contract that I hadn't realized I made. A positive promise for me at that time was "I plan to commit deeply to spiritual practice every single day, no matter how tired I am." That promise was quite helpful so I keep it around.

When you have your list compiled, go through and evaluate which promises you would like to still keep. These are the contracts you will renew for the year. Circle these or mark them out in some way. Now you can look at what's left and take note of all the negative promises, those contracts that are no longer serving you. Cross those out once. Don't entirely blot them out so you can go back and read them later if you become tempted to engage in these negative contracts again. Now your slate is clean you have more room to make better promises filled with intention and grace.

Whispers of the plant world in February

My favorite part of early February is seeing all the new plant life burst forth from the icy ground. In my area, the pending spring is heralded by the arrival of daffodils, irises, daisies, and tulips. The spirits of these plants in particular focus deeply on the powers of happiness and beauty. It's not just because of their delightful colors either! These flowers symbolize the absolute triumph of the Earth's gifts. Their watch-words form phrases such as "I am resilient", "I give second chances", and "I bring the quickening power of spring." These are powerful messages from the plant kingdom we can use to fuel our magick. The gifts of the unique mid-winter plants can be just what we need to get out of a winter slump and give our goals a nice recharge for the second month of the new year.

Exercise – Imbolc quickening plant spell

On Imbolc, gather any plants in your local area known to be early bloomers. I listed the plants in my area above but it is important to use those herbs, flowers, and trees that naturally come alive in the place where you live. As we discussed in our chapter on the element of earth, spirit of place has a great bearing on our magick's ability to flourish and thrive. Even if the only plants you have in your area are new roadside weeds or new shoots of grass popping up in your area, you can use them.

If there is snow on the ground in your area, gather some up in a bowl. If there is no snow, grab some crushed ice from the freezer. For obvious reasons, you'll want to save that until you're ready to work the spell itself. Place the plants next to the bowl of snow and touch both the plants and the snow with your hands. Feel the bitter cold of the ice as it strings your hand. Also feel the texture of the newly-plucked plants. Isn't it amazing that those plants were able to arise and thrive in the midst of that bitter stinging ice? Ponder the power of these resilient plants and silently invite the mystery of their fortitude to flow into you.

Whisper your goals and desires one-by-one into each plant sample and toss it into the bowl of snow. Continue listing goals (or the same goal repeatedly) until all the plant samples are gone and there is a layer of plant matter sitting on top of the snow or ice. Hold your hands over the bowl and with the warming energy of your heart, imagine the snow glowing warm with bright solar energy. Feel the wishes on the plants as words being heated up and dancing about excitedly. When you feel the bowl has been stirred with enough energy, whisper *"by the quickening spring, the goals of my life bring."*

Leave the bowl in an undisturbed place to melt entirely. After everything has melted entirely, you can either pour the mixture back onto the earth or bottle it up as an external potion throughout the rest of the winter

Concerning house magick

Imbolc is traditionally the time for all things home-related. To many Traditional Crafters whose work is very focused on the home and hearth, extra care is put into the workings of the dwelling space. We see this also in many ancient cultures and it's the reason why so many ancient spells consists of charms and spells to protect the home and the family. The ancient Greeks for example placed so much stock in the importance of the home that leaving the house with no one inside it was thought to be the best way to invite ill fortune and death to the family.

Concern for the state of the home on Imbolc makes a lot of

sense for very practical reasons. It's the middle of winter and the least likely time for a lot of people to go outside. Cabin fever (and real fever) find their prime breeding grounds at the start of February. Precautionary measures were put into place to drive these forces away and keep them at bay.

House magick might seem like "low magick" and not of particular interest in the work of diving deeper into one's own spiritual practice in the Craft. But look beyond the volumes of spells and charms and you'll find some of the deepest driving forces that have always pushed humanity forward: love of family. When the home is filled with energy that is abundant and pure, you and your family are able to focus on things like spiritual practice and reflection. Connecting with the spirit of your home is a practice that further aligns you with the spirit of place, for these spirits are not in any way restricted to live only outdoors. Cleaning (both physically and spiritually) and warding are all things you can do to the home around Imbolc that you can see immediate benefits from in both your magick and your life. And frankly, it can be one of the easiest forms of witchery around. So grab that broom and get to work!

Ostara – Spring's arrival

After doing all this work at the start of Samhain to prepare for the dying time, experiencing it, moving through it, and preparing to reclaim the light, we now find ourselves in the season where the light has very obviously returned. It is the vernal equinox near the middle of March and the greenery of the land has really reclaimed its place on the wheel.

Ostara is one of those holidays gifted to us from the Northern European peoples and takes its name from Eostre, the fertile (likely to be Anglo-Saxon) goddess of spring whose dance awakens the spirits of nature and encourages all things to rise up and celebrate. I won't spend too much time going over the traditional imagery of Ostara because even if one isn't familiar with the day in the Pagan sense, they need only look to the celebrations of Easter to see the symbols of the old ways still alive and kicking. Eggs, the hare, and bright pastel colors are all ancient Pagan symbols used to connect to the spirits of fertility and birth.

To the Norse, the goddess Idunn is associated with this time as the keeper of youth and fertility. She is the keeper of the apples that the old gods bite into when they wish to become young again. The connection of apples to Idunn shows an interesting correlation to the forces of life and death and the fine line between the two. One of the Norns, Skuld, was associated with apples and thus we see them viewed as food of the dead. For Skuld in her Valkyrie role was responsible for gathering up the souls of the slain upon death. As we read in the book Gylfaginning from the Prose Edda:

These are called Valkyrs: them Odin sends to every battle; they determine men's feyness and award victory. Gudr and Rota and the youngest Norn, she who is call Skuld, ride ever to take the slain and decide fights.

I point this out to show the careful ebb and flow that these growth/decay holidays maintain. Many of the gods and goddesses of fertility are also highly involved with mythoi connected to death and the underworld. They ride the hedge between life and death, similar to what the spring equinox does as the sun has its zenith over the Earth's equator.

Energetically, Ostara has a very interesting energy and it seems to be a day that some Witches either celebrate with great fervor, or they just don't pay much attention to it at all. I think this could be because Ostara is like the sigh of relief that comes after a long stint of so much bitter cold and darkness. People tend to just be so happy that the days are really starting to get longer that there seems to be little time to interface with the incredible powers stirring at this time. Ostara is the "busy time" when we all rush around trying to get everything done that we could not do over the winter months. Or maybe we could do them all along but we're simply more excited about doing them now. We find that our passion for life has been renewed in a way that encourages us to get out and move. This isn't just all in our head. It's a deep part of our human biology. We were designed to wake up and get out at this time, both for work and for play.

Movement and awakening are the watchwords for this day. In 2006 I attended an excellent Ostara ritual held by the local chapter of CUUPS (Covenant of Unitarian Universalist Pagans). As it was a public rite, I wasn't expecting much in the way of transformative ritual. I was pleasantly surprised to discover that the theme of the ritual was "waking up the earth and our bodies." Together we banged pots and pans, shook tambourines, and shouted across the room in ecstatic dance. Although we cannot know how the ancients would celebrate this day, it seemed like something they would be likely to do.

The seed and origin

In my opinion, the seed is the most glorious symbol for the vernal equinox there is. Not only because late March is a widely-used planting time, but for what the seed itself brings to humanity. In West Sussex there is a frozen underground building housing more than a billion seeds from all over the world. The Millennium Seed Project was started by the Royal Botanic Gardens with partnerships on every corner of the Earth. Their ultimate mission is to preserve seeds from every species of plant on the earth as a sort of "insurance policy" for possible species' extinction. Even after obtaining their billionth seed, they have still only reached 10 percent of their goal. This gives us a vantage point for observing just how important and unique the seeds of the world are.

The harvest is the culmination of all the work we have done. It is what we get before "the end." But the seed holds potential for all that and more. With that potential comes risk. The seed can make it through the growing stage and on to the harvest, or it can fail anywhere along that process. It could even fail by not bothering to germinate at all! Although there are a variety of factors determining the success of any seed, we still don't know exactly why some seeds fail. As an urban gardener, this frustrating mystery brings up a lot of questions both physical and spiritual for me.

When we use seeds in magick, it's usually for work begun at the very early stages of manifestation. If you look at the neopagan customs surrounding Ostara, one of the questions frequently asked of the Crafter is "what seeds are you planting in your life at this time?" This question is more than a novelty. It's a challenge to look beyond our present day circumstances and into the unknown. By looking at myself in the present moment at Imbolc and reflecting on all that I am, I make space to look towards the future, which we really start to manifest on Ostara.

All seed crops demand a certain amount of darkness to germinate. On Ostara, some areas will still be quite chilly and the sun has not yet reached the point where the daylight is stretching on for many more hours. The light has officially "woken up" at this time but its eyes are still adjusting to itself. This sounds strange until we remember that all things in nature, including the primal elements themselves, adapt. This is why this time of year partly challenges us to look at the cold darkness of our past for lessons on how to move forward. Which of our little seeds still have the potential to sprout and grow tall? Which seeds do we recognize as failures and how do we put those failures aside and try again or begin something entirely anew? These are all important questions the spring asks us before we can move forward into the time of the May.

Spring cleaning for daily practice

Ok, this isn't so much cleaning up as it is reorganizing, but you get the picture. With all this talk of putting in the beginning seeds of work, the start of spring can be a fabulous time to shake up your daily practice. Because of the equinox's fertile energy, this is the perfect time to springboard the energy of commitment and focus on our spiritual and magick endeavors. In particular, here are some things to consider:

> Showing up: We will all have time where our daily practice slips. If you've been experiencing that, this is the time to start showing up at the altar again.
>
> Length of time: If your practice has been only ten or fifteen minutes each day, attempt to expand upon this time by adding another ten to fifteen minutes. You can either extend the length of some of your current practices, or add new ones into the mix.
>
> Pull in new creative energy: Are there cobwebs on your altar? Have you maintained the same layout to your shrines and sacred places in the home for a while? Switch things up and give these places in the home a new look.

In addition to any of the above, remember to set new goals for your spiritual and magick work in other ways. As nature all around you is waking up, you can get the creative part of your brain working in a way that refreshes the state of your work. In particular, the following exercise is one I find particularly useful for doing just that.

Exercise – Elemental goal board

Goal boards get replayed a lot in various self-help books and so folks with a Craft background might initially shun them as psychological mumbo jumbo. To be fairly honest, it somewhat is! Organizing our goals and wishes in a tangible way does bring a certain sense of order and rightness to our brain's internal task list. But it does so much more than that. Goal boards, when charged with a Witch's touch, can be an effective long-term spell for pulling things into your life both large and small. For this board, we will work with the elements to engage the natural forces already present in our work.

First, obtain the board itself. I've seen people use cardboard, paper posterboard, dry erase boards, and cork board. I like to use cork board because I can pin and tape things to it with the most freedom to change things up as I need to.

Next, organize your short term and long term goals and desires in the categories elementally which you'll place in the four quadrants of your board. Use your basic knowledge of elemental correspondence to assign the correct element to what you wish to bring into being. For example, my board is currently divided as such:

Air Quadrant: Finish writing this book, complete my review papers at my day job, experiment with new temple incense scents.

Fire Quadrant: Exercise more, schedule more date nights with my partner.

Water Quadrant: Practice my dream magick.

Earth Quadrant: Get more fruits into my diet, reorganize my herb cabinet, plan out my finances for the coming season.

As you can see, my own board is a mixture of goals both magickal and mundane in nature. You can go that route and have them mixed, or you can have one solely related to one area of your life. I also maintain a mixture of goals that are simple and easy (such as cleaning my herb cabinet which I could do in an hour) alongside those that might take me months to complete.

When you have everything all listed out, it's time to start actually posting them to the board. This is a great opportunity to get very creative. Magick is an art just as much as it is a science so the more inspired your board is the better! Again, my own board is a mixture. I have papers pinned that are typed out, hand drawn, and cut from magazines. I also have little packets of herbs and small talismans in each elemental quadrant to give it a boost.

Attuning to spring

The spring air carries with it the vibrations of change, growth, and second chances. When we align ourselves with this energy, we take on the ability to shake off the grip of darkness that had us ensnared throughout the winter months. Attuning to the land at this time forges a connection with your body that can encourage increased energy and drive all throughout the season.

The two equinoxes are quite easy to sync up with. It is a liminal time as the day and night are mostly equal in length, truly unique times among other times in the year. Equinoxes open up a gateway for the complex geomantic forces of nature to flow through. This flow creates a heavy current of power in the atmosphere. This is why many people say they can "feel" spring or fall in the air, unlike summer and winter. It creates a tangible feeling as smells, sights, and sounds all begin to stir and shift around us. The physical act of attuning with spring can be done through formal ritual observance of Ostara as a holiday, or through connecting with the natural spirits directly, which is the method we will cover here. Although you can do this indoors if forced, it's highly preferable to find some wild place in nature to retreat to. If a wild place is impossible, simply being outside on your porch would suffice.

Sit on the ground with your shoes off, feet directly touching the grass, rock, or soil. Initially, perform a tree and roots grounding to enter the correct state of mind. As you breathe, feel the flora all about you begin to wake up and move all about you. The tiny blades of grass tickle your hands and the branches of the trees stretch their mighty branches, as if arising from a long slumber. If it is light out, feel the warmth of the sun on your face and all around you, as if it were gently coaxing everything to get moving. Feel the alchemical process of photosynthesis as the spirits of the sun mingle with and activate the spirits of the green. Notice what this feels like.

Lay the palms of your hands directly on the raw earth just as your feet are. Feel that you are both the sun and the earth combined as you feel that conjoined energy swirl around within you. What parts of you need to be woken up? What needs just a little more space, a little more light, to grow? If answers arise, take a mental note and continue to exist in the presence of this sacred process. Breathe deep in the knowing that this renewal of life has happened consistently every single year since the day you were born and for a millennium before that. Find peace in the knowing that although all things change, stepping into the flow of that change with intention can ease us into the process. Feel confident knowing that you are a master of your own life's changes and can initiate growth whenever it's needed. Sit in this space for as long as you desire and then go about your day.

The above exercise may seem simple but it does carry some profound and visceral energy when performed on or near the vernal equinox itself. After you have done this, you will have a storage unit of springtime energy built up into your energetic field. This power can be accessed anytime you need to begin something new or just need some fresh invigorating energy in your life. You can recall it simply by internally focusing on that deep alchemical process of sun joining earth. This attunement process can be repeated for other events such as lunar works and for various stellar alignment occasions. The point is to ultimately achieve a state where the attunement comes simply from being there once the season turns.

Ostara tree magick

In my local area of the east coast in the United States, the vernal equinox is when I really start to notice the greenery appear on many types of tree. My sinuses notice as well with the onset of spring allergies but I'll refrain from complaining about that here. You could even take a positive approach to seasonal tree allergies by remembering that you're directly connected to nature in a way that other people are not. Trees as beings are most like people when compared to other types of flora. Although many live to be very old, there is an ending to their lives eventually. They "sleep" in their dormant cycles and wake up during this time of year. And most obviously, they allow us to breathe.

The reciprocal relationship between humanity and trees has long been observed throughout the course of human history. Most famously, the modern-day Druids and their forms of tree worship comprise some of the most beautiful tree-based ritual and devotion I've ever seen. Indeed entire volumes of books could be written about the lore of trees and those who love them. For our purposes here, we will specifically be connecting with the great power they bring to the land at this new spring season.

There are many ways to work deep magick with the trees. The common thread running through most techniques involves inter-facing with them in some ways. As we discussed in the earth chapter, dryads are the spirits of the trees responsible for their physical and spiritual functions. Near Ostara, I feel that the dryads of many trees are hard at work performing their many functions from producing new greenery, to working with the bees on pollination. Everything in nature is connected and the seemingly-stationary trees are no different. To work with them magickally, you should first get to know them. If you already have a relationship with a tree near by you, then you have already done most of the work. If not, start speaking to one regularly immediately before moving forward.

It's important with tree magick that we do not physically harm the tree. This is why I like to go with ribbons. Gather ribbons of any color and length with words regarding your deepest soul-level wishes and desires. Unlike the elemental goal board which focused on all goals, the ribbons should regard topics that require a deep knowledge and wisdom, something the trees can appropriately help with. This would be the perfect time to put those magickal alphabets to use that we discussed in the air chapter. I don't know about you, but I wouldn't want my deepest soul-level desires to be available for all my neighbors to see via the ribbons on my front yard's tree. If anything, they'll think of them as a lovely Easter decoration.

So as I've already hinted at above, you'll need to tie the ribbons onto the branches of the tree. Do this as slowly and methodically as possible. Tie them with intention and reverence. This is the way of the trees and they will pick up on your vibration in doing it this way. Speak to the tree as you're doing this and let it know that you'd like to activate these desires by the power of its connection to the emerging spring. You can either leave the ribbons on the tree for the week of the equinox, or keep them on for longer periods of time such as a lunar month or the entire spring season.

Beltane

From April 30 to May 1 we come to what is considered the other "most important" sabbat across from Samhain. Beltane, May Day, Boaltinn, Clain Mai, and Walpurgis Night are just some of the name associated with this day that the ancient Celts considered to be the first day of summer. In many Wiccan traditions, the Goddess and God become fertile at this time and all the earth celebrates the complete and unabashed return of life. Reconstruction religionists of the old Celtic religion will observe Beltane only at the time when the local Hawthorne tree comes into bloom. The word Beltane comes from the Old Irish root words meaning "bright fire." Like Samhain, huge fires called balefires would be lit on hilltops all across the country to celebrate the glory of the fertile earth. Processionals would take place crowning a King and Queen of the May, a tradition meant to mimic the union of opposites.

Beltane is fondly thought of as an exhibitory holiday, largely focused on observing the ancient myths of the gods of the spring/summer with feasting, dancing, and magick for luck and love. In my own tradition at the Firefly House, our Beltane celebrations center around huge potluck feasts, music, and the observation of whatever nature has going on in our local area. This is often a busy time with festivals and handfastings competing for space on the calendar.

With so many outward activities, it can be difficult to remember to travel within on Beltane. We want to leap and dance and have fun with our friends but if we don't take some time to bring the special energy of the day within, then it's just another party. Beltane is an opportunity for us to remember that spinning the wheel of the year means that we take the outward process of changing nature, and sync it up with what's going on inside.

When taking Beltane inwards, we look to the rites we celebrate and see if our internal processes match. The Great Rite, the dancing of the May Pole, and the grand feast are all things we can look at on the inner planes of our souls to dive deeper into the meaning of this day.

The Great Rite

When most people see the Great Rite performed in public ritual, it is what we call "the Great Rite in token." The blade, representing the male life force, is plunged into the chalice, representing the female life force. The reasons this is done in token are culturally obvious, but there is more going on energetically than just the act itself. The conjoining of the chalice and blade represents the deepest acts of integration. The masculine and feminine, the dark and the light, the hot and the cold, all come together to create anew in the spirit of love.

As a queer-identified person, it is important for me to not get caught up in the dualistic gender roles that Beltane often forces people into. For a same-gender loving person, Wiccan observances (and participation) of the Great Rite in token can feel awkward and out of place. And it should most certainly feel that way! Becoming too focused on the flesh and the plumbing is the vice of this holiday. We celebrate our bodies yet challenge ourselves to think about the unique spectrum of energies that comprise us all. After all, every sex contains traits of its apparent "opposite."

On Beltane, the solitary Witch could focus on his or her own brightness and darkness and contemplate how the two speak to each other. How does the experience of one inform the condition of the other? We already know that light does not always equate to helpful and good just as darkness does not always mean that something is cruel or maligned. Taking this into consideration, we can form a helpful relationship with these twin beings that comprise our souls. The shadow work begun at Samhain can be repeated at this time in a way that engages the light half as well. In my own practice, I give my light more room to speak at this time of the year and my dark half more room to speak in the fall. This rotating practice of inviting the different parts of myself to the table of conversation strengthens my presence as a fully self-actualized individual each year. In this way, the Great Rite is not just a ritual gesture, but a process towards a deeper wholeness.

Faerie folk of the May

Beltane is thought to be one of those ideal liminal times attractive to the faerie realm. Whereas at Samhain time the lore surrounding the faerie are arguably more cautious, the May customs concerning the Fair-folk are usually quite lovely. Folklore from the British Isles is brimming with history and lore surrounding the honoring and celebration of the faerie realm. It seems this is connected to the adornments and gifts of flowers given around the first of May, the faeries being thought of as living amongst them and helping them to grow. One of my favorite references to faerie lore comes from an old song that young children would sing in England while caroling door to door:

Good morning, ladies and gentlemen; I wish you a happy day; I'm come to show my garland, because it's the First of May. A bunch of May I have brought you, and at your door it stands; it is but a spray, but it's well spread about, 'Tis the work of the Fays' hands. And now I've sung my little short song, no longer can I stay; Faeries bless you all, both great and small, and grant you a very happy May.

Apart from the joy it brings in celebration of spring in full bloom, I like to think of the May caroling traditions as being possibly connected to the songs of the birds that are heard much more audibly this time of year than any else. Regardless, countless songs and charms like the above show a strong connection to the faerie peoples in these celebrations.

Beltane's power

The start of May indicates a time of great power and passion. These are the watchwords of Beltane. As all the land is exploding with life, so too is the work we began at the start of spring. While I'm not sure that the power itself is in more quantity at Samhain and Beltane, the sensory experiences of it are certainly more palpable at these times.

Working with the power adrift on the air of May Day brings deep joy and satisfaction on a soul level. Generally, most people tend to be in better moods by the middle of spring. This could either be because of the newly-warm air, the increased light, or the excitement of dreams for the summer. Either way, Beltane's power rests in the knowledge that at least for the time being, we can celebrate our joys and cheer our successes.

Tapping into the power of Beltane's current can gift our

magick with the spirit of encouragement. Even when our goals are in the process of manifesting, it can be easy to ease up on the commitment we're giving to our work and our desires. At times when it feels like life is just peachy and there's not much else to do, we celebrate what we have done. The vice of Beltane however is resting on your laurels. Victory and celebration is very healing, but we mustn't ignore the work of the soul. As an exhibitory holiday, we need to hone in on the joy all around us and bring it inwards to contribute to our continued success. The birds know this. In the midst of their courtship and mating, they are also preparing by building nests and finding safe and secure homes. They find a balance point between the needs of survival and the need to thrive.

Exercise – Beltane bird magick

Every species of bird each has its own unique medicine that it contributes to the world. The crow embodies knowledge and the mysteries of death. The hawk is the messenger of the gods and brings insight to humanity. But all birds share a few things in common. With their flight, they symbolize the spirit of freedom and the sheer joy of being untethered. The true spirit of spring and of air makes itself known by the miraculous flapping of their wings. They also nurture and their concern for nesting shows a deep abiding love for family and security. Both freedom as well as restraint are powers of the birds and of Beltane itself.

For one week (preferably the week before Beltane itself), look to the ground in your daily walking for things that could be of use to a nest. Bits of twigs, string, fluff, etc. Each time you spot something like this, take it up and store it away. Do this every day for a week and (depending on where you live) you should have a decent collection of nest materials. If your collection is scarce, you can go out and grab other bits of twig and sticks sought intentionally. Let the process itself be part of the work, not just a means to an end. Going back to faerie lore, it is believed by many that little shiny things left on the ground are token gifts from the spirits of nature and should always be picked up and taken home. You can think of the things you pick up for this rite in a similar way.

Once you have everything collected, enter sacred space with your nesting materials along with some glue and a basket. Place everything on the altar (or just on the ground before you if outside) and become comfortable. As you breathe, observe the sounds of the birds chirping away. If there are no birds making noise, imagine what that would sound like right now. As you breathe into your core take note of those things within you that would benefit from bird medicine. What within you craves freedom? What needs to be nurtured and coddled a bit? As you hold these feelings, begin to glue the different materials into the inside of the basket, working from bottom to top. If you'd like to sing an incantation, you could use something like this:

I am the spirit of birds and the song of spring
my wings expand to take in the gentle air
All within me is in process
all without me nurture's my becoming
The sun of the May is my beacon
and all of nature turns to its brilliance
Come alive, oh spirits of feather and fey
and nestle close in this basket of May.

When all the materials are used, the working is done. You can continue to add found nesting materials throughout the rest of the spring and make the basket more cushioned as time goes on. Although the creation of the basket itself is its own working and will cause immediate changes within you, you can use the basket as a tool to hold various prayer and spell papers as needed.

Litha

Also called Midsummer or simply Summer Solstice; Litha marks the height of physical power in terms of the journey of the sun. Of course its position in June opposite of Yule means it is the light-half of the two solstices. If Yule holds the spirit of promise, then Litha holds the spirit of fulfillment. Magickally, Litha is seen as one of the most powerful times to perform magick of any kind, especially when connected to solar or fire-based pursuits. The sun reigns supreme at this time and all things under its domain are blessed and empowered.

So many polytheistic cultures observed the Summer Solstice that it would be impossible to cover them here. But the common threads of connection between many of them center on vitality, strength, and the full expression of one's own power and the power of the gods. At Litha, our personal pursuits begun six months ago would certainly be showing signs of manifestation, if not fully manifested already. Internally, we check ourselves to see what could use more strength. Although brute force alone is not enough to make things happen, it can sometimes be a helpful thing to get us to the finishing line.

Litha's enchantment

Due to the sheer amount of raw power adrift on the air at Litha, this solstice is thought to have an almost intoxicating influence on humans and animals alike. Again we find another sabbat highly connected to the lore of the faery realms. Those not familiar with Paganism in any capacity will likely still be familiar with Shakespeare's *A Midsummer Night's Dream* in which the fey play a role. Again, this would be due to the "thin veils" at this time of year.

One of my first teachers told me to look at the dynamic of Litha's energy as a type of enchantment. The blazing sun, the long days, and the many social parties can make time seem to speed up. To me, it is the time of daydreams and lounging under a big tree with a book. The warm summer air both day and night is simply enchanting. My coven's tradition, Firefly, is named after the alluring image of the lightening bugs that bop up and down in the fields and suburbs in our local area around this time. It is trance-induction by nature alone and what I believe to be one of the greatest forms of enchantment.

In late June, take time to stop and sit outside at various intervals. Observe the way the things look now as opposed to how they were in the May. Marvel at the explosion of green among the trees and the speedy tasks of any small animals that might be running about. Take this time to daydream without restriction. Allow yourself to become totally entranced by the natural world. Write down what comes to mind later in your journal. Observing the crossover into summer can lead to greater knowledge in summing up enchantments down the line. The visceral feeling of the new summer can become an instant trigger, granting us quick access to deeper power.

Exercise – Drinking the sun

This is a rite that can be easily adapted for either solstice, although I usually feel more drawn to perform it in the summer. The rite that I call "drinking the sun" is at its most basic, a libation. At its most complex, it's an invocation. In many ways it's both. Toasting to the sun and moon is nothing new to many Witchcraft traditions, although it usually seems to be only part of a larger rite rather than the focus of one. The purpose of drinking down the sun is two-fold. First, it's an act of alignment with solar energy. Through sympathetic magick, we attune the beverage to the power of the sun and then take it in to become part of our internal system. The second reason is that the act of libation honors the gods and the spirits. Thus the rite honors the power that you're taking in, creating a symbiotic relationship between you and them.

The only tools needed for this rite are a cup and a beverage.

The style of cup doesn't matter but the drink should be one that has some solar qualities to it. Citrus drinks like orange juice or even lemonade are perfect for this. Fresh and organic is best if that's possible. It would also be preferable to be outside or at least in some quiet place in the home with a view of the rising sun.

Be seated with your beverage in the cup on the early morning of the solstice. Spend a few moments looking in the direction of the sunrise, feeling its warmth fall upon your skin. Breathe deep and begin to feel power building in your body and in the cup before you. Know that the way the sun charges your body directly will be different than the way it will charge you when drinking the sun. The alchemical process of light charging liquid which will then feed your body connects with the deepest mysteries of Earth fertility and the nourishment of the land. Contemplate this as you continue to feel the power build. When you feel like the light has reached an apex within you, take up the cup and hold it before the sun. Feel the two merge into one thing. Imagine that the drink has literally become solar flame, potent and alive. Then drink it all down. Although I usually sip it slowly as I meditate, I've also chugged it down for a more visceral feeling within the body. The rush of charged sugary liquid makes for an interesting high sensation and can feel like downing a couple of shots of espresso. Either way, this rite should leave you with a nice glow throughout the day which can be of great benefit to any other magicks performed through the remainder of this sabbat.

Rising to the light self

If the precursor to Yule is focus on the shadow self, then the advent of Litha would be focus on the light self. Again with many magickal traditions we see a strange oversimplification when talking about the light self. The simplification of shadow self is that it is somehow evil or maligned, but what of the light self? Light self's bad rap comes from the idea by some that bringing light into one's being is "fluffy", "woo woo", or otherwise unfit for a true adept of the arts. Of course this is also untrue and ignoring this work can create the same sort of imbalances that can occur if shadow is not greeted and integrated.

Some might say that the light self is the "higher self" operating on a more expansive vibration than the shadow self. In my experience, I don't feel that the light or shadow selves can be entirely arranged on an ascending/descending scale. Just as the shadow can live within the realms of the bright lands, so too can the light self descend into the depths. Instead, it feels more helpful to equate this part of ourselves with the solar mysteries that accompany a holy sun day like Litha. Litha itself is not a state of eternal brightness. With its wild celebrations comes the sobering realization that after today, the light will once again begin to decrease. The apex of brightness is so fleeting that it almost seems as if the light itself is tethered to its own shadow. And in a way it is. They are what the Feri tradition of Witchcraft would call "Divine Twins", dual powers that are both opposites and equals. They both battle and make love all at the same time and from their encounter emerges oneness with self.

The light self is everything embodied by the sun and the "upper worlds". In music it would be the high notes that peak at the crescendo of the world's best masterpieces. It is the part of us that craves expansion and freedom. Like the sun, it wants to be at the center of all things. It wants to be seen, loved, and craved back. When we come into conversation with light self, we become like the alluring lover on the edge of a potential kiss. We embody the feeling of "butterflies" in an excited belly. And best of all, we become a source of illumination for our own lives.

Rising to the light self is simply the act of living all of those qualities and breathing them into being. Attuning to the powers of the solar cycles can do this, but so can casting a glance on a morning sunrise, or saying a prayer at the high of mid-day. Notice your place in the revolution of the sun and know that like it, you are in process. You are becoming.

Lughnassadh - The first harvest

At last we return to the time of shadow. The sun, just leaving its height of heights, is beginning to set in the west. We still feel the joys of the warm summer air, but know there is much work to be done. As the first harvest, Lughnassadh (or Lammas) was the grain harvest that came before anything else. At this time, all the grain in the field was harvested save for one final sheaf at the end. This sheaf of grain was bundled together and fashioned into a doll. The doll was said to literally hold the spirit of the harvest within it, so great care was taken in its preparation. This really represents the spirit of what the start of August must have meant for ancient farming communities. The seriousness of the harvest was tempered with the joy of this interesting tradition of making a doll.

We take the name Lughnassadh from the Celtic god Lugh. As a solar god of strength and skill, he embodies all that the first harvest is, both internally and externally. On the outside, he is the game-maker and the joy that comes with the annual harvest festivities. My own coven observes this with the playing of games of skill each year. On the inside, he is the somber reminder of the dying time and the coming of darkness. He is a god of sacrifice and challenges us to take ownership of the work we did throughout the year, for good or bad. Energetically, Lughnassaadh has the ability to hold things together and weave things into place. Its opposite sabbat Imbolc shows some similarities to this as a day of weaving and homecrafting. But this day is more focused on the community and one's relationship to the outside world. It asks us to observe the dynamics of our family and those close to us. Which of those relationships do we want to nurture? Which will likely fall to the side, and how will that affect our work? Even if a Witch is not outwardly a member of any specific community herself, she can still be affected by the deeds of those around her. So Lughnassadh then becomes a time for the work of refining and clearing in addition to the already busy work of pulling helpful things in.

Living the harvest today

Why do we even bother observing the harvest when most of us can walk into any grocery store in the middle of winter and buy fresh greens or anything else we desire? Is the harvest even relevant to the urban or suburban Witch in particular? Those questions bring about some very interesting debates all across modern Paganism today. They're questions that speak to our current situation as a society so detached from the cycles of nature, that nature itself can be seen as a distant romanticism. While I agree that the idea of celebrating a harvest when most of us don't harvest food can be good for the psyche, I also think it does so much more than that.

The first harvest is the gentle preparation for more work to come. Although there's work to be done, it's the kind of work we're excited to do. It's the feeling you might get spiritually when engaging in a new daily sitting practice layout, starting a new job, or beginning the next phase in a long-term project of any kind. Don't be fooled into thinking that the harvest is an end. The year's cyclical nature ensures that each season is both a starting and an end at the same time. Lughnassadh provides us with a wonderful opportunity to look at the work we've done so far and make whatever changes we need to for the future. We've come so far, but do we dare pick up the spear of Lugh and plunge back into the game? Can we extend our reach just a little further into the depths of our potential?

Journal on these questions and see what answers arise. It's ok if you don't feel the need to get much more out of what you're working on right now. Mastery and rest is important, but do take this opportunity to challenge your current position. Take a breath, then move through the work.

Exercise – Rite of the Golden Grain

For thousands of years, grain has been a symbol of life for so many countries. In times of great need when bread was just about all you could afford, wheat was a savior to the people, the enemy of hunger. We're not talking hundreds of years ago either. Think of the great depression and the bread lines, all less than a century ago from the time of this writing. The goddess of the grain spins and courts her lover, even though she knows the time for his departure is nearly here. Her spinning brings forth all the blessings of the first harvest, the first full bellies after a long day's work. She ensures we have what we need and a little more. The god of the falling grain becomes, in essence, the beginning results of our efforts. In invoking this divine dance, we can use the power of Lughnassadh to connect with our goals to gain a new perspective. We use this as a mile marker to cultivate a greater sense of success and in doing so, a greater strength for what comes next. Materials needed:

3 stalks of wheat (wild-picked, in a seasonal market, or even from a craft store if necessary)
1 yard of red string
A yellow or golden candle

As you begin to come into a place of stillness and meditation, think of those parts of you that need a little encouragement. If there is any area of your life or your work that could be helped by validation from your soul and the gods, what would it be? What requires skill to be brought into fullness and completion? Let these thoughts simmer about in your mind as you take up the wheat stalks. Hold them close to your heart as you say:

I am the farmer of my life's work. No one but me can charm the golden grain from its soiled slumber. No one but me can reach for the midway sun when the darkening approaches.

Oh you fertile gods of the harvest, come and witness the ripening of my spirit! As the spirit of the golden grain bows in response.

Braid the three stalks together and feel the richness of the harvest encircle the space around you. Take in the sweet scent of the burning sun and feel it nurturing the essence of your work. *Become* the grain as you tether your aspirations to the material plane by way of the wheat in your hands. Then light the candle and take up the spring. Charge the string to bind the intention by holding it above the flame (but not close enough to catch fire) and say:

The gods of destiny do weave the threads of my life. Clotho, Lachesis, Atropos; Let the spinning of the wheel merge my intent with the power of this day. Let the turning of this season bring me strength and skill. The blood-red cord confirms the power and seals my charm. So mote it be.

Slowly wrap the string around the braid of wheat, still contemplating the things you're bringing in. When the wrapping is done, so is the rite. Allow the candle to burn down and lay the wheat braid on the altar or some other area in the home that gets a lot of use. You can even keep it under your bed to encourage the incoming energies to merge with your being.

Mabon

As we circle back towards our starting position on the wheel, we come to Mabon. Placed on the autumn equinox near the end of September, Mabon is another liminal time, sandwiched between the first and final harvests. Many Neopagans lovingly refer to it as "Pagan Thanksgiving" and in many ways I'm inclined to agree with that. Although it's the second of the harvest festivals when observing the Wiccan calendar, it really *looks* much more like harvest festival than the one preceding it. Obviously, it's the first day of fall with its opposite day being Ostara. Once again we find the balance between night and day, light and dark. This time, the dark is winning and the days are visibly becoming shorter every day.

With the quickened waning of the light, we look again to the stories of the descent goddesses. In the spring time we saw the return of Persephone from the lands of the Underworld. At this time, Persephone's time on Earth is finished for the year and she begins to make her way back down to join her husband as the Queen of Death. In her mourning, Persephone's mother Demeter plunges the Earth back into the cold as the fruits of nature begin to wither and die. The descent theme is echoed in other cultures such as the story of Inanna who made a similarly perilous journey to the depths. Inanna's story is sometimes thought of as more grave, as she physically died while receiving the violent scourge of her dark sister Ereshkigal. In all these autumnal descent myths we see a great journey of a god who emerges transformed on the other side. As a result, the Earth is transformed. It's no wonder why so many areas of the ancient world revered the fall season with a sacred respect and deep admiration.

The arrival of the fall is symbolized by the image of the full cornucopia. The cornucopia likely originated from the horn of the river god Achelous which was ripped off by Hercules. The horn was given to Abundantia and thus immortalized as a symbol of plenty. The hope of having more than enough to survive is at the heart of the September harvest season. We all want to know that at the least our basic needs will be met. I've often thought this might be the same feeling that intrigues some to begin a practice in Craft. Through Witchcraft, we can expand our expectations and feel comfortable with wanting more. In our harvest observances, we celebrate what we have because we know there is room for so much more.

The spirits of autumn

The fall season is filled with marvelous stories of spirits and gods who fill a number of important tasks. The most notable of course would be the Corn King or Harvest King who prepares for a self-sacrifice that will provide food for the people through winter. His symbolic sacrifice points to the cycles of death and regeneration that take a noticeable turn at the autumn equinox. We especially see this in the ballad poem of John Barleycorn by Robert Burns, a metaphorical story of man as grain being killed for the season. Towards the end, he is regenerated as beer and lives again.

There was three kings into the east,
Three kings both great and high,
And they hae sworn a solemn oath
John Barleycorn should die.

They took a plough and plough'd him down,
Put clods upon his head,
And they hae sworn a solemn oath
John Barleycorn was dead.

But the cheerful Spring came kindly on,
And show'rs began to fall;
John Barleycorn got up again,
And sore surpris'd them all.

The sultry suns of Summer came,
And he grew thick and strong;
His head weel arm'd wi' pointed spears,
That no one should him wrong.

The sober Autumn enter'd mild,
When he grew wan and pale;

His bending joints and drooping head
Show'd he began to fail.

His colour sicken'd more and more,
He faded into age;
And then his enemies began
To show their deadly rage.

They've taen a weapon, long and sharp,
And cut him by the knee;
Then tied him fast upon a cart,
Like a rogue for forgerie.

They laid him down upon his back,
And cudgell'd him full sore;
They hung him up before the storm,
And turn'd him o'er and o'er.

They laid him out upon the floor,
To work him further woe;
And still, as signs of life appear'd,
They toss'd him to and fro.

They wasted, o'er a scorching flame,
The marrow of his bones;
But a miller us'd him worst of all,
For he crush'd him between two stones.

And they hae taen his very heart's blood,
And drank it round and round;
And still the more and more they drank,
Their joy did more abound.

John Barleycorn was a hero bold,

Of noble enterprise;
For if you do but taste his blood,
'Twill make your courage rise.

'Twill make a man forget his woe;
'Twill heighten all his joy;
'Twill make the widow's heart to sing,
Tho' the tear were in her eye.

Then let us toast John Barleycorn,
Each man a glass in hand;
And may his great posterity
Ne'er fail in old Scotland!

As we discussed earlier, the last crop of the harvest is said to embody the spirit of all the harvest itself. The final corn was ritually cut and fashioned into a corn dolly which was either kept for the entire year, or just until the spring planting season. I find it interesting that depending on the area and the people, the harvest spirit was seen as either male or female. We have either the sacrificial god who throws himself under the scythe or the fertile grain goddesses who oversee and blesse the entire process. Even in Wicca where many things are polarized into one gender or the other, the sacred autumnal duties are shared by both goddesses and gods alike. It seems to add to the feeling of equity and reciprocity that both equinoxes bring. The spirits of autumn initiate the union of "opposites" for the common goal of plenty.

Besides the corn and grain, we also find a few specific fruits that play a strong role in the harvest and deity descent lore. The apple in particular is beloved by many gods and finds itself at the center of too many myths to mention here in great detail. As the prized fruit of the Norse goddess Idunn, the apple is seen as a symbol of immortality in the face of impending death. So much so that the gods maintained their immortal status by feasting on the gifts of Idunn's orchard. Similar to Idunn but differing in personality is Pomona, the Roman orchard goddess. Although Pomona loves all trees, apples are her favorite, winning her a prime spotlight among the prime beings of autumn.

Finally, there are the many male gods of the fall. Lugh, the Green Man, Pan, and Dionysus are among the more famous. Dionysus in particular does well to represent the spirit of autumn with his reputation for blessing the wild fertile places like orchards and fields. Although he's best known as a god of grapes and wine, he was revered for general vegetation much earlier.

Dionysus teaches us about the wild mirth that the fall season can bring. In many Pagan traditions when something is called "Dionysian", it's based on the exhibitory and ecstatic practices. So through Dionysus, we learn that the dying time of nature can also be a cause for celebration and wild revelry as well.

The power of abundance

There is a term in US contemporary Paganism known as "Poor Pagan Syndrome." That is, the strange view that most Pagans don't make as much money as other people or that we're not willing to give money to projects and causes we care about. In some cases this is true, but not any more than other people in what we call a "bad economy." I've always wondered how this cultural stigma came about. I sadly don't know the name of the brilliant person who said "a poor magician, is a poor magician." If we are truly practicing effective magick, then it should be obvious that we would have all that we need and more. I believe the problem arises when we enter what's called poverty mind. Poverty mind is a state of lacking and need in both the physical and mental sense. And since this mindset is present in the physical and mental, it slowly finds its way into the spiritual bodies as well.

Being the main harvest of the sabbats, Mabon calls us to

examine if we're in a state of abundance or poverty. I believe this is of utmost important to Crafters as we must have our basic needs and the needs of our family met before we're fit to deal with our Craft. As Witchcraft is a system of personal responsibility, we already know that no one is going to do it for us. We must open our arms and call out to our future blessings, seen and unseen. Part of that is gratitude for what we have, but it must extend further than that.

The Witch who is aligned with abundance has a mindset of confidence that he would not have otherwise. She knows exactly what she needs and what she must do to get it. If obstacles stand in her way, she simply dissolves them one by one and moves on. If resources or connections are lacking to get the desired thing, he will call those resources to him on the winds, or in the surge of the rising ocean tides. The Witch who is aligned with abundance has a daily recognition of the abundance of nature and seeks to emulate that abundance in every step and word. In doing this, we open ourselves to greater connection to the fertile earth and limitless sky.

Money isn't dirty unless we make it that way. Prosperity does not corrupt the soul unless we allow it to throw us out of alignment with our True Will. Money is not good or bad, it's just energy that we can do with what we please. It's up to us to decide if we'll use it for success or discord. Personally, I prefer success!

Exercise – Mabon abundance jar spell

It's important to remember that abundance does not always mean money, so it's good to keep a clear vision of the type of abundance we wish to attract. You might need to simply attract cash, but you might also be in need of love, friendship, networking connections, or any number of things required for personal success. This rite will attune you with the fruitful energies of Mabon so should be performed on the day of the equinox itself or the day before. This working will mimic the

cornucopia as a twist to the traditional Witch's Jar spell.
Materials needed:

1 large glass or porcelain jar

Handfuls of autumn leaves of any color, preferably form a tree
on your property

At least three of these herbs: nutmeg, cinnamon, cardamom,
allspice, cinquefoil, chamomile, rosemary, and dried
orange peels

Dried fruits of any kind (raisings and apples are especially
appropriate)

Orange candle

Pen and paper

Perform this spell outside if possible. If you must be indoors, it
would be helpful to sprinkle some of the leaves about you in a
circle. Have all the materials before you as you begin to breathe
deep and find your center. In your center you sense a tiny
autumn sun, glowing hot with all the fall colors of the leaves
before you. On each breath in, the little sun begins to expand
until it encompasses your entire body. Burning brighter again, it
continues to expand and eventually forms the entire circumference of your circle. Know as you are seated inside the core of
the sun itself, you are within the super-machine of our solar
system that makes all life on Earth possible. You sense the gentle
rotation of the planets around you. You feed them light as they
reflect their glow back to you. Light the orange candle and lift
your arms up slightly to your center, palms up. Call out to the
goddess of abundance:

Abundantia, Lady of Plenty, salutations to thee
Bright maiden of the turning Earth, with colors wild and bright
You sing the gentle melody that expands the ripening fruit
Your earthen touch brings forth life from the barren soil

Oh Queen of yearning desire, attend this rite and extend your blessing
For the hour of the equal standing is upon us, and I open to receive it.
Abundantia, I bid thee welcome.

Take up the leaves and sense the spirit energy of the tree they fell from. Silently call out to the tree spirits to aid you in the work of bringing abundance to your life. Stuff them into the jar. Then take up your chosen herbs and spice and mix them together either in a bowl or in your hand. Repeat the tree procedure but call out to the spirits of the plants to lend strength and power to the spell. Sprinkle the herbs into the jar as you say:

Blessings of the harvested Earth
Mix and mingle and come forth for this work
Instill within and around me, the spirit of abundance
Let all the spice of life be mine to have and hold
Sweet smelling gifts of nature's bounty, I summon, stir, and conjure.

Take up the dried fruits in your hand and repeat the procedure of calling out to their host spirits. I prefer the raisins and apples due to their strong mystical reputation with the gods of abundance and fertility. These will be used as the offering to the gods.

On the sheet of paper, write out exactly what you wish to create abundance towards in your life. It's important to be specific here because abundance goes both ways and isn't always lovely. After all, you can have an abundance of credit card bills or an abundance of spiritual crises, and we certainly don't want any of that. I find it helps to style the request as a letter to the gods, and perhaps to Abundantia specifically if you worked to establish some sort of prior relationship with her.

Lay the dried fruits unto the paper and roll the paper up. If the paper ends up being taller than the jar when rolled up, you can fold it or do whatever you need to do to make it an appropriate size. Insert this into the jar and say:

Oh you mighty gods and spirits of the harvest
Accept this offering, the fruits of bright miracle
The weakening sun burns bright within me and calls out for your
  blessing
Take of these gifts and let the cycle move on
In the shade of the coming winter, I take your hand and walk in
  plenty.

Close the lid tight on the jar. Drip some of the wax from the orange candle around the lid and sides of the jar to energetically seal it further. Unlike the traditional Witch's Jar used for protection and banishment, you shouldn't bury this. Instead, keep it in the kitchen or a central place in your home. You'll have the abundance you seek for the next year, although you'll need to replace the jar at Mabon of next year.

In conclusion

Remember, the wheel of the year and all the sacred feast days contained within it are both literal observances as well as outward expressions of internal occurrences. Celebrating holy days is one thing, but the Witch looking to go a bit deeper will take in the wheel itself. He will align with and internalize it on every level. It becomes a part of us, and us a part of it. We spent so much time discussing the days of power because they present us with frequent opportunities to unite with the mighty forces that rule the tides of our everyday lives. Both practical and mystical, Witchcraft's transformative power presents itself fully when worked with every day of the year.

Chapter 9

Putting it All Together

We have arrived at the point where we should be grounded in a deeply meaningful practice. Through the elements, we learned to align our bodies and develop meaningful relationships with the spirits of nature. With the gods, we learned how to co-create an existence for ourselves that is fully human and fully divine. And as we danced the wheel of the year, we synced our souls with the rhythms of our sacred Earth and all within. Although I've outlined methods for deeper connection in many areas of the Craft, you can take anything discussed in this book so much further. And you should. That's where the beauty and power of Witchcraft lives. In the constant possibility to expand the container of our practice. The reason why the Craft has such limitless potential is that humanity does to. As one of my teachers T. Thorn Coyle says: "We are always in a state of movement. But we can move towards evolution or devolution." When it comes to the direction of our lives, we have a say in the matter. Sure all of this is deeply spiritual, but it's deeply practical as well. Witches spend so much time working with the Earth and the natural elements because we are of the Earth and (at least for a time) live directly within it. We cannot separate the magickal from the mundane because each one is also the other. In the end, nothing is fully magickal or fully mundane. Our container – which can be helpful for the work of discerning boundaries – can limit our sight and cause us to forget that all things are made up spirit. It is the Witch's job to see beyond the veil of what looks to be there. She craves to know more, to have more. When we identify these external things around us as manifestations of spirit, we remember that we are as well. This remembering is perhaps the greatest act of integrating power. The work in this book can be used as a full system on its own, moving through the core exercises and rituals throughout the course of a year. But more importantly, it's a road map that I hope will assist you in deepening your practice as you go. As you moved through the work here, I hope you identified areas that could have been expanded upon or explained more. What would you have added? Take that internal feedback and use it to expand your practice as you see fit.

No one but you can engage in the magick of transforming your life. Take a breath, take a step forward, then make it happen.

In Her Name,
David Salisbury – October 1, 2012

Bibliography

Adler, Margot. Drawing Down the Moon. Boston. Beacon Press, 1979

Angeles, Ly De. Witchcraft: Theory and Practice. St. Paul. Llewellyn Publications, 2000

Buckland, Raymond. Doors to Other Worlds. St. Paul. Llewellyn Publications, 1993

Buckland, Raymond. The Witch Book. Canton. Visible Ink Press, 2002

Cabot. Laurie. Power of the Witch. New York. Bantam Doubleday Dell Publishing, 1989

Conway, D.J.. Magick of the Gods and Goddesses. Berkeley. The Crossing Press, 1997

Coyle, T. Thorn. Kissing the Limitless. San Francisco. Red Wheel/Weiser, LLC, 2009

Cunningham, Scott. Cunningham's Encyclopedia of Crystal, Gem, and Metal Magic. St. Paul. Llewellyn Publications, 1988

Dominguez Jr., Ivo. Casting Sacred Space. San Francisco. Red Wheel/Weiser, LLC, 2012

Fortune, Dion. The Mystical Qabalah. San Francisco. Red Wheel/Weiser, LLC, 1935

Grimassi, Raven. The Witches' Craft. St. Paul. Llewellyn Publications, 2002

Grimassi, Raven. The Wiccan Mysteries. Woodbury. Llewellyn Publications, 1997

Huson, Paul. Mastering Witchcraft. New York. Penguin Putnam Inc., 1970

K, Amber and Azrael Arynn. RitualCraft. Woodbury. Llewellyn Publications, 2006

Leland, Charles. Aradia or The Gospel of Witches. Newport. The Witches' Almanac, 2010

McCoy, Edain. A Witch's Guide to Faery Folk. St. Paul. Llewellyn

Publications, 1994

Parma, Gede. Ecstatic Witchcraft. Woodbury. Llewellyn Publications, 2012

Roderick, Timothy. Wicca: A Year and a Day. Woodbury. Llewellyn Publications, 2005

Pearson, Nigel G.. Treading the Mill. Milverton. Capall Barn Publishing, 2007

Penczak, Christopher. The Living Temple of Witchcraft, Vol. 1. Woodbury. Llewellyn Publications, 2008

Palin, Poppy. Craft of the Wild Witch. Woodbury. Llewellyn Publications, 2004

Roob, Alexander. Alchemy & Mysticism. Los Angeles. Taschen, 2006

Starhawk. The Spiral Dance. New York. Harper and Row, 1979

Stone, Merlin. When God Was a Woman. Orlando. Harcourt Brace and Company, 1976

Starhawk. The Twelve Wild Swans. New York. HarperCollins, 2000

Walker, Benjamin. Beyond the Body. Boston. Routledge & Kegan Paul Ltd., 1974

Wolfe, Amber. Elemental Power. St. Paul. Llewellyn Publications, 1996

Moon Books invites you to begin or deepen your encounter with Paganism, in all its rich, creative, flourishing forms.